PARENTING ESSENTIALS

EQUIPPING YOUR CHILDREN *for* LIFE

ANDREAS AND MARGARET
KÖSTENBERGER

CHRISTIAN
FOCUS

Copyright © Andreas and Margaret Köstenberger 2020

paperback ISBN 978-1-5271-0538-6
epub ISBN 978-1-5271-0595-9
mobi ISBN 978-1-5271-0596-6

10 9 8 7 6 5 4 3 2 1

Published in 2020
by
Christian Focus Publications Ltd,
Geanies House, Fearn, Ross-shire,
IV20 1TW, Scotland, Great Britain

www.christianfocus.com

Cover design by Pete Barnsley

Printed and bound by Bell & Bain, Glasgow

As parents of five children, my wife Ann and I have learned that modeling a close walk with God and leading our children to a vibrant relationship with Him is no small feat. Andreas and Margaret give a biblically robust yet simple framework to keep us on track as parents. Our family has been encouraged as we've watched them become more like Christ while their children have become more like them and so have become more like Christ. May this be true for each of us who read and apply the experiences they share in this book!

DAVE MILLER
Church Planter, Leadership Coach, Great Commission Business Owner,
Oklahoma City, Oklahoma

Sleep-deprived, anxious, and uncertain about the daunting task of successfully raising a child to adulthood, new parents can't help feeling overwhelmed. And that's just in the first week. The glut of advice online only adds to the insecurity. Enter *Parenting Essentials*, a practical, readable, faithful guide through the sometimes perplexing, often fulfilling, and always sanctifying work of parenting. Andreas and Margaret Köstenberger serve well as older believers (Titus 2) and long-time parents faithfully teaching younger believing parents how to nurture children to adulthood in the strength that God supplies. Their aim is more than the common goals of graduating from college, getting a good job, and becoming responsible citizens. They offer practical help for each stage of development while keeping their focus on the overarching goal of parenting according to God's design, by His grace. Andreas and Margaret give parents a vision for what's possible when you look to the wisdom of the One who created the family and gave parents the responsibility to bring children up in the fear of the Lord. Even though our youngest is nearly finished with elementary school, we're glad to have *Parenting Essentials* for the years still ahead of us on our parenting journey.

STEVE AND CANDICE WATTERS
(Respectively) Director of communications, Truth78.org;
Author of *Start Your Family: Inspiration for Having Babies*

This is practical, biblical counsel for Christian couples in all stages of parenting. It is positive, detailed, and exceptionally insightful teaching that is always supported by Scripture. The authors' conservative approach offers needed help to parents who want their family to follow Christ and resist the destructive forces of culture. There are specific suggestions, helpful summaries, and good questions for further consideration in each chapter, so a small group could study the book together with great benefit.

GARY AND ANN WOOLEY
Founders of Marriage Plus International, Denver, Colorado

A great read—practical, biblical, and spiritually challenging.

JOSH MOODY
Senior Pastor, College Church, Wheaton, Illinois
President and Founder, God-Centered Life Ministries

My parents wrote this parenting book. Spoiler: they're regular parents. And while they aren't perfect, they sure did care for and invest in me. My dad used to get home from work and practice pitching baseballs with me until it got so dark outside we couldn't even see each other anymore. He's patient, generous, and works really hard. Whenever we couldn't sleep for whatever reason, my mom would sit by our bedside and sing us songs until we fell asleep. She's caring, creative, and industrious. Regardless of any mistakes they may have made, I knew both my parents really loved me and they instilled a love for God in me. I turned out alright if I may say so myself—so give this book a read. I think you'll find it to be an invaluable resource for you as you cope with your crazy kids. All that said, I give this book the official child-approved stamp!

DAVID KÖSTENBERGER
Son of Margaret and Andreas Köstenberger

CONTENTS

From Us To You

You may be a young couple who recently had your first baby and are asking yourselves: What have we gotten ourselves into? Or you may be going through premarital counseling and are looking forward to your life together which, you hope, will include having children. Perhaps you already have several young children and are feeling overwhelmed. Maybe you're simply looking for what you hope is another useful book on parenting, knowing there's always more to learn. You may be a single, widowed, or divorced parent who is looking for ways to be a better parent, or an experienced parent or couple who is looking for a good parenting book to use in mentoring or to give to your own adult children.

Whatever your situation, and whatever your purpose for picking up this book, we want you to know that we share a vital bond because, like you, we care deeply about parenting. We believe that being a parent is one of the greatest joys, privileges, and responsibilities with which God has entrusted us.

Sadly, however, we live in a culture that in many ways diminishes the role of a parent and the task of parenting. Often the not-so-subtle message is that a career or some other avenue of self-realization is superior to the so-called dull and dreary drudgery of changing diapers, doing the laundry, and taking your children to an endless litany of ball games, piano recitals, and dance lessons. In many other ways, the role of parents is disparaged in our world today.

Yet the world desperately needs parents who engage in parenting that is *realistic, relational,* and *responsible* (3R parenting). We need moms and dads who embrace their God-given role as parents with humility, grace, commitment, a sense of stewardship, love, and a healthy dose of humor. Over the years, raising four children has brought immense joy and occasional grief. Being a parent has been exhilarating and excruciating. In the words of Charles Dickens, it has been 'the best of times' and 'the worst of times.' Yet we wouldn't exchange the joy of being parents to our children for anything. Nothing can compare to bringing a new life into the world and then over a couple of decades nurturing that young life, by God's grace, slowly but surely into mature adulthood.

The 3 Rs of Parenting

Well, then, let us tell you a little bit about this book. In this (hopefully) engaging and accessible volume, we seek to introduce current or prospective parents to the three Rs of parenting: *realism, relationship,* and *responsibility.* Each of these emphases is borne out by a tension we perceive especially in young parents: between idealism and realism; between relationship and task orientation; and between responsible engagement with your children and a permissive stance. Within this framework, we propose an approach to parenting that accentuates the need for realism, a focus on relationship, and taking our responsibility as parents seriously, especially during our children's most formative years.

Tensions in Parenting

Tension	Proper Parenting Emphases (3 Rs)	Parenting Weaknesses
1	Realism	Idealism
2	Relationship	Task Orientation
3	Responsibility	Permissiveness

Many, like us, start out their parenting journey with great hope and boundless enthusiasm, only to gradually awaken to the messy and challenging reality of life as a parent. Others feel inadequate and are unsure if they're up to the task. While bringing up children isn't easy, we believe that parents can absolutely rise to the challenge! Adopting the values and proposals we present here in a spirit of hopeful realism is sure to make a difference in raising children who aren't characterized by rebellion, foolishness, and unwise decision-making but exemplify joy and maturity in growth, eventually identifying marriage partners for life along with a personal calling.

At the outset, we'd like to ask you a simple question: *What's your goal in parenting?* Truth be told, many—even those who've been parents for many years—never take time to formulate their parenting goals or reflect on their parenting philosophy. We didn't either—at first! As a result, we do the best we can, but many of us 'fall' into parenting (as one might 'fall' in love) and probably aren't as effective as we could be if we consciously developed parenting goals and objectives. But what should our goals be and how should we seek to accomplish them? In this little book, we hope to provide a *framework* laying out God's design for parenting. In this way, you won't find yourself constantly reacting to the latest crisis or disciplinary issue but instead act out of your God-given identity and role as a parent in keeping with God's larger purpose for you in Christ.

About This Book

Now, you may wonder: Who are the authors of this book? We're not parenting experts, but parents like you. We're not professional speakers who travel the worldwide lecture circuit to talk about parenting. Nor are we professional counselors who can draw on a long case log of people who have come to them with their parenting problems. We're a Christian couple who believes in mentoring and making disciples. We love God and love the joy and the challenge of being parents. We love God's Word and what it says about marriage and the family, and we dearly love our children—not as some form of idolatry but as God's unique persons, gifts for us to cherish and to help develop for Him.

You may also ask: How is this book unique and distinctive? In short, it's written not by an individual man or woman but by a married couple—both a mom and a dad *together*—who've had the joy of raising four now-grown, thriving children. As you read this book, you'll hear both of our voices interwoven with each other—male and female, husband and wife, father and mother—in a way that reflects the partnership (and occasional struggle to move toward a unified perspective) that we believe is so vital in parenting.

Also, we embrace a *biblical-theological approach*, that is, we seek the Scriptures from beginning to end to see what they can teach us about a given topic—in our case, parenting. That is, our approach is not primarily socio-cultural (focusing on dry family structures and traditions), psychological (dealing with emotions, honing communication skills), or counseling-oriented (addressing problems in sexual sin, drug addiction, rebellious teenagers, etc.).

While we touch on some of these issues along the way, they are not our *primary focus*. Instead, we seek to construct a firm *biblical foundation* for parenting, based on who God has revealed Himself to be in His Word and on the purpose for which He created us as human beings in His image—male and female, and as parents. In doing so, we hope to help parents be proactive and hope to help them avoid some of these counselling issues that typically arise in today's family.

Not that we've done a perfect job—far from it. However, we've learned a few parenting lessons and have tried to make the necessary adjustments along the way. Hopefully you'll be able to do a better job than we did as you're equipped with some of the practical and biblical insights we have learned and share in this book.

Parenting with Perspective and Purpose

Primarily, we've written this book to help young couples gain *perspective* on the entire parenting process so they can parent with a coherent *purpose*. While many young couples start out with lots of idealism and live largely in the present, facing the challenges as they come, much can be gained by understanding the *life cycle of parenting*: from infant to toddler, all the way to the teenage years and young adulthood. Also, we want to assist young couples to develop a *parenting vision* that's inspirational, comprehensive, and holistic. This will help you to fill your sails so you can fulfill God's calling for you as parents, and you'll be equipped to parent with perspective and purpose.

Rather than stumbling along or moving aimlessly through the maze of the parenting landscape, we're convinced you'll benefit from parenting with purpose and perspective. To help you do this, we'll try to help build a *realistic* framework for parenting. You'll learn more about the importance of viewing parenting as cultivating a set of—at times messy, but infinitely rewarding—relationships: parents with children, and children with God. You will hear us issue a clarion call not to abandon your children to the high winds and torrential waves of the culture! Otherwise, don't be surprised if they're spiritually tossed around or even swept aside by the currents of our times. Few assignments in life are more rewarding than helping a child develop a sense of mission, calling, and a connection with God and others in this world.

So, are you ready to join us as we explore the joy-filled lifetime journey of being a parent according to God's design? Come on, then, let's get started!

Part 1

REALISTIC PARENTING

Waking up to the Real World of Parenting

Having a baby can be a great, fun adventure. It all starts with the exhilarating discovery that you're pregnant. This exciting news is all a young couple needs to dream about starting their own family. They tell their parents and friends, and maybe post the good news on social media. They buy a new crib—or borrow a used one—and start decorating a room for the new arrival or wait until they know the baby's sex to choose the appropriate color scheme. Little time is spent thinking about the challenges that lie ahead. This isn't the time for realism—it's the time to dream and celebrate, especially if the couple has been planning to have a baby for a while.

Nine months later (after weeks or months of nausea, weight gain, and other possible discomfort, to be sure), the baby is finally born. A new life has come into the world! Those of us who have witnessed the event will agree that few experiences can compare with the wonder—the miracle—of seeing the birth of a baby. The family rallies around the young couple, and shortly after the birth, mother and baby come home, perhaps to streamers and balloons and a *Welcome Home*! sign. Now it won't be long till some cute baby pictures are being posted on Facebook, and perhaps an announcement is sent to family and friends. It doesn't get any better than this. The Bible pronounces marital bliss on the two who enter marriage and become one. Now the two have become three. A married couple has become a family, and all is well.

Or is it?

The baby, it turns out, isn't always as sweet as in those initial pictures. In fact, if she's hungry or thirsty, or often for no apparent reason at all, she bursts out crying. As a young parent, of course, you try to troubleshoot as best you can and attempt to figure out what the problem is. Chances are, the baby is hungry. Or, he or she is tired and needs to sleep. Or maybe there is gas in their tummy. The list goes on and on. There will likely be some sleep deprivation, and many unsolved mysteries. No matter how hard you try, having a baby can't just be reduced to a science or a few simple steps. Welcome to the perplexing world of parenting!

Things won't always go perfectly in those first few weeks of parental 'bliss.' As a young couple, you may be able to take those early struggles in stride: You've read a few parenting books, talked to experienced parents, or even can call on a supportive network of family, friends, and a local church community. Yet the tension invariably mounts, and a gap opens—slowly but surely—between rosy-eyed idealism and rough-edged realism. Your baby may have instant reflux (as one of ours did), and you may spend the first six months of their young life struggling to feed them enough to help them thrive. Or, you may encounter other challenges that send you to the internet, the family doctor, or leave you bewildered and at a loss for what to do.

Parenting takes sacrifice. You'll be called to sacrifice your sleep, your energy, your time—and good intentions are rarely enough. It'll take more than dreams of family happiness to make it through those tough spots. Those who are unaware of how complex parenting can be, and how different it is from what they imagine it to be in their ideal world, will most likely experience a measure of conflict and disillusionment because challenges are sure to come. Are you ready? Or are you already in over your head? Like other challenges, parenting can bring out both the best and the worst in us. Raising children is one of God's ways of building character in us, driving us closer to Him and to each other.

1
The Parent

As you begin this chapter, take time to reflect on the fact that parenting starts with parents. The person you are makes an enormous difference in the life of your child, because we tend to reproduce after our own kind. Also, begin to embrace the truth that the mission of parenting is given by God at creation and is grounded in the fatherhood of God.

> ♦ *Read Genesis 1:26-28, Ephesians 5:1-2, and 1 Corinthians 11:1. What can you learn from these foundational passages about the role of the parent?*
>
> ♦ *Read 1 Thessalonians 2:7-12. What can you learn from this passage about some distinctive roles of father and mother?*

What's the first thing that comes to your mind when you hear the word 'parenting'? Chances are, it's not 'parents' but 'children.' Parenting is all about children, right? It's about disciplining them, getting them to behave the way they should (or at least the way we want them to so they don't embarrass us in front of our friends and relatives); it's about nurturing them, providing for them, protecting them, and preparing them for life. Well, *of course* parenting is about children. Without children, there'd be no parents. But at the same time, without parents there'd be no children! And what's true in the natural realm is even truer in the spiritual realm: The key to a child's physical and spiritual development lies primarily with the parents. *Thus parenting, properly conceived (pun intended), starts with the parents.*

So, that's where we'll start our exploration of parenting: with ourselves, the parents. What role do parents have in parenting? First, parents have only got themselves to 'blame' for the quandary they're in, correct? One important reason for this is the foundational principle of reproduction, which is this: *We tend to reproduce after our own kind.* Like it or not, our children often do as we *do*, not as we *say*. The best way to come close to producing the kinds of children we want, therefore, is *being* those kinds of people ourselves. Let's not make this too complicated.

At the same time, there's no shortcut to parenting. And the parenting process is as messy and complex as walking with God every day and keeping in step with the Spirit. In addition, new responsible relationships pile on top of existing ones with every child that is born. So, as we become more like Christ, and as our children become more like us, they, too, will become more like Christ (not to take away our children's individual responsibility). Or the opposite will be the case: If we *don't* follow Him, our children's character will likely deteriorate as well. We realize we're running the risk of sounding simplistic here, but all things being equal, it really *is* that simple: Like father, like son; like mother, like daughter (Ezek. 16:44). So if you want to do your children a huge favor, pursue your relationship with God (He is of course worthy of your love and worship in His own right). This may mean getting up earlier, spending less time on social media, or playing less golf—but it'll be vital to becoming the parent God wants you to be.

Created in God's Image

Marriage is the foundational institution on which parenting is built. God created us not only for community and for relationship, but specifically for *male-female partnership*. In this way, we're called both to enjoy each other's company and even sexual intimacy, but to our point here, we were created to participate in God's work in this world through having children! The Bible says, 'God created man in his own image ... male and female he created them'. And He told them, 'Be fruitful and multiply and fill the earth and subdue it.' Later, Scripture adds, 'Therefore a man shall leave his father and his mother and hold fast to his wife, and they shall become one flesh' (Gen. 1:27-28; 2:24).

In a nutshell, this is God's plan for humanity. Through sexual union, and the children that are born, we partner not only with each other but also with God in reproducing new image bearers for His glory. Amazing! Children are a blessing from God, and a reward from Him (Ps. 127:3-5), not only because they are so adorable, but also, and more importantly, because in them we fulfill God's calling for us to reproduce and fill the earth with other human beings who bear His imprint and likeness. Parenting, therefore, has an important theological (God-related) dimension.

So how does this translate to parenting? A Godward orientation invests parenting with great significance. We have the privilege of reproducing ourselves in the form of beings who, like us, bear God's image. This is truly a privilege and responsibility worth embracing. Grasp this reality and live it out! Parenting is so much more than the daily grind of keeping your children in line and getting them to the places they need to go. Bring up your children in the fear and admonition of the Lord, and be mindful of the larger God-sized purpose of glorifying Him in the way you raise them. Endure, persevere, and keep your eyes on Him.

As a Christian, keep in mind that your children are bearing the image of God and reflect His glory to the extent that they honor Him with their lives. Your mission as parents, to a significant extent, is therefore to help your children realize that at the very heart of their life's purpose is to glorify God as the unique individuals He has created them to be. Therefore, aim to instill in them their uniqueness and purpose from God. Remind them that God has fashioned them in a purposeful way and that there's no one exactly like them.

Your children have amazing, God-given potential to use everything they've been given for Him, and they need to be regularly reminded of this. Their gifting, their interests, their education, and eventually their vocation—all are specifically designed by and spring from the God who made them. Help them to live the adventure of a life aligned with

God's purposes specifically for them! To the extent that we neglect to see our role as parents in this larger, God-centered perspective, we miss out on His full plan and purpose, and fail to allow God to receive the glory He so richly deserves.

Grounded in the Fatherhood of God

There's also another important dimension and privilege to parenting. Those of us who enter the joys and trials of parenting can experience more fully a dimension of the Godhead that would otherwise remain less familiar to us. We're talking about the fatherhood of God, which is the foundation for all human parenting. Consider the following affirmations in Scripture: 'For this reason, I bow my knees before the Father, from whom every family in heaven and on earth is named ...' (Eph. 3:14-15). Here we see that God is the source or origin of every family that exists, and parents, in procreation, enter spiritually into experiencing what it means to be creator.

And, 'we have had earthly fathers who disciplined us and we respected them. Shall we not much more be subject to the Father of spirits and live?' (Heb. 12:9). Here we see that as fathers and mothers, we can relate to God on a deeper level because we can further enter experientially into what it means to be sustainer, provider, protector, and ultimately parent.

Above all, then, the very notion of parenthood is grounded in *God* and who He is as *creator*: He is 'the Father, from whom every family in heaven and on earth is named.' On this basis, the apostle Paul prays the following prayer for every member of the church 'that according to the riches of his glory he may grant you to be strengthened with power through his Spirit in your inner being, so that Christ may dwell in your hearts through faith—that you, being rooted and grounded in love, may have strength to comprehend with all the saints what is the breadth and length and height and depth, and to know the love of Christ that surpasses knowledge, that you may be filled with all the fullness of God' (Eph. 3:16-19).

Now, please reread this prayer one more time with your parenting in mind, realizing that Paul at the beginning of this passage invokes

God as the 'Father from whom *every family*' is named. Therefore we can appropriate this prayer for ourselves as parents and pray it for our children as well.

Think of it! *As parents*, we can be strengthened with God's power through His Spirit in our inner being so that Christ may dwell in our hearts through faith; and that, grounded in love, we may have strength to comprehend the profundity of God's love for us *and for our children* that is really beyond comprehension—a paradox—so that we may be filled with all the fullness of none other than God Himself! What's more, we can pray the same prayer *for our children*: that God may grant them to be strengthened through God's Spirit and to deeply know God's love for them. Parenting could be transformed if we were to adopt this perspective and pray this prayer for ourselves and for our children.

Now please read the second passage we touched on above regarding parenting: 'It is for discipline that you have to endure. God is treating you as sons. For what son is there whom his father does not discipline? If you are left without discipline, in which all have participated, then you are illegitimate children and not sons. Besides this, we have had earthly fathers who disciplined us and we respected them. Shall we not much more be subject to the Father of spirits and live? For they disciplined us for a short time as it seemed best to them, but he disciplines us for our good, that we may share his holiness. For the moment, all discipline seems painful rather than pleasant, but later it yields the peaceful fruit of righteousness to those who have been trained by it' (Heb. 12:7-11).

Again, it's obvious that we should conceive of parenting as grounded in God's own essential being and role as Father. Specifically, this realization and reality have the potential of transforming our experience and exercise of discipline on our children. God, the author asserts, disciplines His children—that is, believers—out of love. It's because of His love for us that He disciplines us the way He does. He disciplines us because He cares for us very deeply.

While in this passage, the author uses human parenting as an illustration for the way God acts as parent, he also affirms the kind of fatherly love we should have for our children. Ultimately, God's love is exemplary: We should take our cue from the way God loves and cares and disciplines. What's more, the entire analogy presupposes that there's an affinity in nature between God and earthly fathers—that as fathers, we reflect the way God acts as our Father.

What flows from our reflection on the fatherhood of God, therefore, is that parenting isn't merely a matter of external effort and method but rather a God-reflecting approach to loving and caring for and discipling our children that can only work for *Christian* parents and fathers. It's a characteristic spiritually grounded in the new birth that all believers have experienced at conversion. Only *regenerate* parents, therefore, can reproduce the kind of parenting—though never perfectly (as sinners)—that is characteristic of that exhibited by God. This reflection on the nature of God thus allows us to see more clearly foundations for our parenting.

By extension, what is said about the fatherhood of God and about the role of earthly fathers also applies to *mothers* because parenting is a stewardship given jointly to both the man and the woman, with the man as the spiritual leader.

The Man as Spiritual Leader

Apart from the fatherhood of God and the fact that we're created in God's image, there's another important foundational reality that is necessary to understand in developing our parenting philosophy. This reality is the fact that, in marriage, God has appointed the man to a role of spiritual and functional leadership and has brought the woman alongside him as a companion and compatible partner (Gen. 2:18, 20).

Throughout Scripture, the man is shown as called to work and provide for his family, and to lead his family (as well as God's people, where qualified men are appointed to this role in the church; Gen. 2:5-9, 15-17; 3:17-19; 1 Tim. 3:4-5). The woman is shown to be called to a primary role in relation to her husband and children, one which involves devotion to making the home a nurturing and supportive environment for her family (Gen. 3:16, 20; 1 Tim. 2:15; 5:10, 14; Titus 2:4-5). In all of this, the man and the woman together partner in 'exercising dominion,' that is, taking care of God's good creation, in large part, in and through the God-given family structure (Gen. 1:28).

The loving complementarity, in which the husband is a Christlike, sacrificial leader and the woman his gracious, compatible partner, is vital both for a God-honoring relationship which is in keeping with God's original vision and design but also as a basis for effective parenting (Eph. 5:21-33). In this way, a couple models a biblical male-female relationship to their children and this pattern undergirds their parenting. The family—both wife and children—look to and respect the man's role to lead and love sacrificially, and father and mother work in tandem as parents.

What's more, getting back to God's design and order means for father and mother to exercise proper dominion over their family, including their children. Not only should the man and the woman be rightly related to God and to each other, they should be rightly related to their children. In God's plan, raising children is *our* responsibility! We shouldn't farm them out for someone else to raise them. The world says: Delegate the care and education of your children to others; give them independence; send them away. God says: Exercise proper dominion as those created in my image—for my glory. Train, care, educate—be present with your children!

When a disciplinary issue arises, the husband is called upon to take the lead. When important decisions are to be made, again it is incumbent upon the husband to take initiative in leading through the decision-making process, though of course he would be remiss not to carefully consider his wife's wishes, input, and opinion on the matter. Often it will be the mother who needs to follow through on the discipline of the children when the father is at work, but even there she'll do so based on previously established principles and ultimately deferring to her husband's leadership in the Lord.

In our experience, Andreas typically establishes broad parameters and gives overall direction to our family and our children. He sets the vision and exercises broad oversight. I'm integrally involved in many practical specifics, such as finding a suitable curriculum for school, identifying options for sports, music lessons, discerning needs, and so forth. That said, both of us are involved *together*; Andreas doesn't just delegate the children's education to me wholesale and remain completely aloof from it. We're partners, and both of us stay actively engaged.

For the man to act as the leader, he must genuinely care and be continually involved. There's also a need for effective communication and agreement on a course of action, both in casting a vision and in specific decision-making. There may be a certain division of labor, but ultimately, we're in this together. And in the infrequent cases where we can't agree, I defer to Andreas's judgment. Most times, he is very reluctant to go against my judgment, though, because he has come to trust my instincts even where his mind might tell him otherwise.

Hopefully, this gives you a basic idea of what a marriage of complementarity might look like in practice where the husband is a maturing spiritual leader, the wife is growing to be a wise and intelligent partner, and the couple is exercising joint dominion over their children and family. We believe we allow God to work more powerfully through us when we embrace God's ordained roles and identities for us—in principle, from the heart, and in the day-to-day practical challenges of marriage and parenting.

Parents as Sinners

To be theologically grounded and oriented in our parenting, it's crucial to understand yet another aspect of what it means to be parents, and it is this: It's not only children who are sinners and thus need guidance and correction—parents are sinners, too! We're far from perfect. In fact, we're fallen and in need of redemption. In everyday life, we might suppress this knowledge and live as if we're essentially good in our human nature and disposition, or at least attempt to do so in our own strength. We try hard to do the right thing, and to be good parents, and maybe there are even times when we seem to succeed. But is this *real* success or the dangerous *illusion* of success? Often, it may be the latter.

Remember the *reality* of what we're dealing with. As Jesus once said, without Him we can do nothing (John 15:5). Conversely, in Paul's words, we can do all things through Him who strengthens us

(Phil. 4:13). Yet while Jesus and Paul didn't *specifically* apply these truths to parenting in these passages, we believe that they most definitely do, even especially so.

How does the realization that we—the parents—are sinners affect our identity and role and practice as parents? First, even though we're to imitate God in our role as parents, we're not God. We can, and will, make mistakes—plenty of them. So, when we do, we should in all reality and humility accept responsibility and apologize to our children asking for their forgiveness. We should humble ourselves and not use our position to lord it over them or coerce our children. This is huge! We should encourage and nurture our children as responsible agents and decision-makers, equipping them to accept responsibility for their own actions and decisions by our own example.

It's easy to start out the day with good intentions, but it doesn't take long before our children begin to wear us down and our patience grows thin. We gradually get more and more exasperated and may even eventually blow our fuse. That's it! We've had enough! And we feel like throwing in the towel. The problem is, as parents we can *never* throw in the towel (if we try, we'll have to pick it up again!). Running away from being a parent is never a realistic option. Even though our children may have done something wrong, we're still responsible for the way we respond. Fussing, complaining, or even yelling at our children in anger is a temptation, and when we succumb to it, we certainly owe our child a sincere apology. They, of course, will learn from this when they themselves experience their own sinful limitations.

It's extremely important as parents to be mindful of the fact that we're sinners. Parenting can be demanding and trying on a person. Especially for the mother who is home during the day with young (or teenage) children with little support, her character is being constantly refined. In view of this, it helps to acknowledge the limitations we both have as parents regarding our finite frame and specific personal weaknesses, not to mention the fact that we're sinners by nature. We should live in the light of these truths and expect that there'll be times of challenge and conflict. Try to be proactive; prepare the whole family for the likelihood of conflict. We all will likely fall short in one way or another.

Redemption in Christ

That's why we must work out our parenting—like our salvation—with fear and trembling (Phil. 2:12-13). We've seen how God created the man and the woman to exercise joint dominion over creation, with the man as the leader and the woman as his compatible partner. We've also seen how the Fall affected men and women not only generically but specifically in their male-female roles and identities. So, how does redemption in Christ relate to our roles in marriage and family?

First, in receiving forgiveness of sins, we also receive the *Holy Spirit*, and are enabled to live a new life of faith and obedient submission to the lordship of Christ. Second, we are *reconciled* to one another, and *forgiveness* is always available when we fall short. Third, redemption in Christ has not only ramifications for us as individuals or for relationships in general; it makes it possible for God's *original design* for man and woman (including parenting) to be *restored*.

No longer do the man and the woman need to blame each other or others (whether God or Satan) when things go wrong. No longer does the man need to abdicate his God-given leadership role or the woman act on her tendency to control her husband. Rather, as both are individually filled by God's Spirit, they're enabled to relate to each other as redeemed people in Christ (Eph. 5:18). The wife can trustingly submit to her husband in the Lord, respecting him and affirming him in his role as leader of the marriage and the family (Eph. 5:22-24).

The husband can love his wife sacrificially, caring for her and for his family selflessly and indefatigably as he was originally created to do by God (Eph. 5:25-29). There can again be pulling together, rather than being pulled apart, as the man and the woman are united as partners in exercising dominion over the earth as God's representatives, specifically in their roles as father and mother as they raise and shepherd their children.

Fathers will serve as loving *providers* and *protectors* while mothers will serve as devoted *nurturers* and *partners* in parenting their children alongside their husbands. In this way, God's order will be restored in His image. Conversely, where parents, and fathers in particular, fail to exercise dominion, there'll likely be *disorder, disunity*, and *dysfunctionality*, if not *confusion* or even outright *chaos*.

In addition, parenting has an important trinitarian dimension—taking place in union with *Christ*, by the power of the *Spirit*, for *God's* glory—as the man and the woman bring up their children in the nurture and admonition of the Lord. Nevertheless, living according to God's original design will often involve apologies and extending forgiveness, starting with the parents. This process will prove redemptive and bring healing where there is brokenness and strife.

Importance of Parental Unity

Let's, therefore, talk for a moment about the importance of parental unity. As mentioned, the Fall divided the man and the woman; and redemption made it possible for father and mother to be united again. This points to an important component in parenting: the *marriage*. The saying has merit that the best thing a man can do for his children is love their mother (and vice versa). Time and effort invested in a marriage can vitally affect our success in parenting. I recently met with someone who confessed to me that he and his wife had had terrible conflicts over how best to parent their oldest child from his wife's previous marriage. Hours were spent in fruitless discussion, and in the end, they still didn't reach agreement on how to enforce house rules, methods of discipline, suitable friendships and activities, and just about every aspect of parenting. Not only did that make parenting virtually impossible, it also put a severe strain on their marriage. This confession bears powerful witness to the importance of parental unity in raising children.

My wife, like most mothers, is passionate about instilling wisdom in our children. In principle, I certainly agree. In practice, however, consensus in the past has at times proved elusive. One of the important questions we worked through early on in our marriage and in beginning a family was regarding schooling. Should we send our children to a public school, a Christian private school, or school them at home? Friendships were another vital area of discussion. Which friendships should we encourage, and which ones should we discourage? What about certain movies or watching shows on television? Vacation? Should we go to the beach, especially with young and growing teenage sons when there are many scantily dressed young women putting their physical beauty on display? The list goes on and on.

It's hard enough for our children to navigate the treacherous waters in this beautiful yet fallen world; it's even harder if parents are unable to speak with one voice. As a couple, we've spent countless hours talking through various issues. We're grateful to testify, to the glory of God, that over time we've become much more united in our perspective on parenting than we've ever been. Parenting is arduous work. In fact, it's total commitment—to each other, to our children, and to God. In our case, differing views sometimes depended on differing maturity levels at the time of discussion. Other factors included different personalities, backgrounds, or in some cases personal preferences. Acknowledging these legitimate factors is sometimes hard but extremely valuable in working through differences. The time you spend in conversation with your spouse talking through parenting issues is vital. It truly is time well spent.

Please, listen to your spouse and to his or her concerns. Generally, try to trust each other's intentions—that both of you have the best interests of your children at heart—even if you're initially miles apart in what you think your children should be or do. Men, trust your wife's general intuitions. I've often found that my wife's instincts were far ahead of what I could cerebrally or rationally grasp about an issue or person. I could cite many examples which taught me that wives have discernment and concerns about potential influences in our child's life, and even if I can't see the relevance and deem them harmless or disagree, I typically heed her words of caution, especially since she is a wise, and spiritually mature woman. You'll be very glad if you do, too.

Conclusion

The person you are makes an enormous difference in the life of your child. So, don't take any shortcuts in this aspect of parenting. Don't believe parenting is all about your children, about taking them places, giving them experiences, managing their successes in school—their grades and their education—even their friends. Parenting is first and foremost about *you*. You have the privilege of living out God's original design for you as parents. As husband and wife, partner to bring up your children in the nurture and admonition of the Lord for *God's* glory, in *Christ*, and by the power of the *Spirit*. *You're the parent from whom parenting flows*! Parenting isn't just a *task* that is performed irrespective of the *person* exercising it. Think of parenting as moving organically from God to parent to child:

$$\text{GOD} \rightarrow \text{PARENT} \rightarrow \text{CHILD}$$

As parents, we'll reproduce after our own kind. We'll typically reap what we sow. Therefore, we should not only pay attention to the God-ordained role given to us but to our personal relationship with God and our own character. If my husband is driving carelessly, he shouldn't be surprised if his children—especially my sons—pattern their driving after his. If I'm worldly in the way I dress, or talk about other people behind their back, most likely my daughters will follow suit. Remember, children typically do as we do, regardless of what we say. So, parents, let's allow God's character transformation to start with *us*. Then we'll have plenty of time to parent our *children*, and chances are, they'll listen a lot more and turn out a lot better than if we neglect our own personal and spiritual development and approach parenting in isolation from it.

♦ *Reflect on and discuss your expectations for your family. What are your fears, hopes, and dreams and how can you assess these considering biblical realism?*

♦ *Considering what you've read in this chapter, do you think your expectations are realistic and biblical? How can you live out your God-ordained role as parents, mother and father?*

♦ *What do you need to work on in your relationship with God and in your personal life to be better equipped as a parent?*

2
The Child

No matter how adorable, children are sinners, born with a sinful nature which cannot be reformed but must be redeemed. Though we love our children deeply, we should be careful not to idolize them. Read the following passages and begin to reflect on the vital role of parental discipline, encompassing both positive guidance and correction. Later, you'll read more about how fathers, in tandem with mothers, are primarily responsible for disciplining their children.

> ◆ *Read Genesis 3:1-7. What went wrong at the Fall, and why? What we can learn about life after the Fall from this passage?*
>
> ◆ *Read Genesis 3:9-13, 16-21. How did God act as a parent in the aftermath of the Fall? What can we learn from the way in which God treated His children when they sinned?*

It's truly a joyful occasion when a baby is born to an exhilarated couple! Sooner or later, though, as we've already said, reality settles in. As this lovely baby grows, he or she appears to be focused almost entirely on himself/herself. As toddlers, they often refuse to share their toys. They may pout, hit, or scream when they don't get their way or may throw a tantrum. Soon, the realization becomes inescapable: Every child, no matter how adorable, is a sinner. This simple yet profound insight is vital for effective parenting: The sinful nature cannot be reformed; it must be redeemed. No amount of discipline can replace regeneration of your child.

Children Are Adorable, Aren't They?

We still remember when one of our children was observed to be telling lies in second grade, and their teacher called us to talk to us about a specific incident that had occurred. Apart from feeling slightly embarrassed that *our* child was lying, not just once but apparently repeatedly, and this not just in the protection and privacy of our home but in the public arena of the school, we were puzzled: How could our child not be more truthful? After all, we had taught our children the value of honesty! Mercifully, the lying turned out to be more of a phase than a permanent affliction, but God used these difficulties to impress on us the one simple fact: Our child, too, is a sinner in his or her own right! And this manifested itself not only in general terms but in concrete, wrong actions that could ultimately be traced to their sinful nature.

'For all have sinned and fall short of the glory of God' (Rom. 3:23)—including that delightful little one you're holding in your arms! I know, you may not want to hear this, but while it may be an inconvenient truth, it's still true. Just as an aura of mystique surrounds a man and a woman 'falling in love,' it seems that a similar cloud of romanticism hovers over a newborn baby, regardless of the faith commitment of a given couple. A cognitive dissonance however soon develops: We love the masterpiece of our own flesh and blood we created, but we sometimes (often?) hate the things they do and the grief (or at least inconvenience) they cause.

Theologians speak of 'original sin' (Catholics) or 'total depravity' (Protestants). David in the Bible wrote, 'Surely I was sinful at birth, sinful from the time my mother conceived me' (Ps. 51:5). Like it or not, the sin of Adam and Eve in the Garden affects all of us, whether or not we think it's fair that we have to suffer for what others did centuries before us. God knows, if we'd been there, we likely would have done the same thing: disregard God's instructions and do things our way.

Children are sinners. We need to let that sink in. What this means, then, is not only that children *sin*, but that they are *born with a sinful nature*. They have an innate tendency to sin, a bent toward sinning (which, by the way, doesn't alter the fact that they're responsible for their actions). We can't see inside our children's hearts but based on what we know about their sin nature, we know that pretty much everything they do will be motivated not by love for God, or love for others, but by love of self. They can't say no to themselves and have little self-control in their own strength. They're little manipulators—and they're skilled at it, too! In fact, over time the child develops the art of manipulation to perfection, so much so that they've got you convinced that they love you, and do what they do, out of love for you. In return, you'll likely do everything in your power to make and keep them happy. Oh, if it were that simple. But as we all know, eventually sin rears its ugly head and destroys the happy picture.

So, don't trust all the family pictures—perfectly posed, all smiles— you see on social media. (We're obviously not suggesting you post unpleasant pictures). Beneath the surface, though, there's frequently relational pain and a continual struggle with sin.

Alternatively, some may deny that sin even exists. Or maybe you're somewhere between these poles on the spectrum. Why do we, at times, deny the reality of sin, when plainly not all is well with humanity, including our children? And why do we think children are somehow exempt from this universal malady—sin—that plagues humanity? Not only does the *Bible* attest to this fact, there's also ample *anecdotal evidence*. So why don't we start believing it and act accordingly?

Parenting and Idolatry

As parents, we should start out our journey with a healthy dose of realism. Otherwise, we're likely in for a major disappointment—or a series of major disappointments—and will likely not thrive as parents, with unrealistic expectations on ourselves and our children. We may end up being too harsh in discipline or be tempted to overlook the need for correction. Rather than indulging a parental ideal of a sinless and adorable child, only to be rudely awakened to the reality that beneath the sweet smile lurks a sinner just like the rest of us, we can cultivate a more measured appreciation and love for our children that resembles God's disposition toward us. As God's Word tells us, 'God so loved the world that he gave his one and only Son' (John 3:16 NIV); and again, 'God shows his love for us in that while we were still sinners, Christ died for us' (Rom. 5:8). He calls parents to do the same—love our children, knowing full well that they're sinners.

This reality—call it original sin, total depravity, or brokenness—is not merely a helpful insight, but a bedrock, foundational conviction that should undergird all our parenting efforts. Once we honestly acknowledge the reality of our children's sin, we'll realize more fully their need for consistent, loving correction. Though the merely external intervention of correction is necessary, as we've seen earlier, acknowledgement that by itself it will be insufficient to address the root problem, our child's sin nature. For this, we'll need the Spirit's assistance—dependence on Him to convict our child that they're sinners and to provide the means to be saved from their bent toward evil and from their tendency toward rebelliousness and disobedience. This, in turn, requires much patience, prayer, and persistence on the part of the parents.

The Root of the Problem

Sometimes, as parents, we just want to address the immediate problems we face with them—our child's misconduct. That's understandable, but somehow, we never get around to coming to terms with the underlying reality: the continual bent toward sin we have been talking about. How should we understand this proclivity toward evil? As the Bible puts it, 'All we like sheep, have gone astray; we have turned—everyone—to his own way' (Isa. 53:7). Sometimes, our children don't blatantly disobey (though often they do). Instead, they may employ more subtle ways of resistance. Like sheep lacking a strong hand, they meander. They drift, gradually veering off the path into precarious territory. Extrapolate this over the course of several years (if not decades), and you have wayward teenagers hardened into rebellion and then into adults that occupy a position diametrically opposite to where they should be—morally, vocationally, and spiritually.

So, then, rather than merely treating symptoms, let's get to the root of the problem. While children are small, they may or may not be able to understand the concept that they're sinners deep down inside. But as they grow, we should gradually alert them to the fact that there's something inside of them—their bent toward sin—that makes them do the things they do. They'll find within themselves the very same reality the apostle Paul describes: 'For I do not understand my own actions. For I do not do what I want, but I do the very thing I hate' (Rom. 7:15). What we as parents need to understand, then, is that not only does our child choose to disobey, he or she isn't truly free *not* to disobey because of his or her innate bent toward disobedience.

All too often, however, we operate in our relationship with our child on the premise that he is perfectly capable of obeying if he simply chooses to do so. The problem with this notion is that it presupposes that human nature is essentially good, or at least neutral. Some of you reading this chapter may not be convinced of the Bible's teaching regarding sin. In fact, there's a strong liberalism and romanticism in our culture that says people can choose their own destiny—or at least they should be able to—unencumbered by interference from anyone else. However, this notion of a truly free person is a myth. Don't base your parenting on a utopia. You can only work within the realm of the reality that exists. You and your child will be better served to face the truth and deal with it, to the point of your child recognizing and receiving the gift of salvation and the ability to live a life of holiness in dependence on the God who has provided this for all of us.

The Necessity of Disciplining Our Children

Why and how should parents discipline their children? In the everyday hustle and bustle of parenting, few issues are more important. And yet young couples are often at a loss—and older couples, too—as to how to administer discipline in keeping with Christian principles. As sinners (especially young ones!) and as those who are in the process of being spiritually formed and trained (Proverbs calls young people 'naïve' or 'simple'; 1:4, 22, 32; 7:7; 8:5; 9:4; 14:15, 18; 21:11; 22:3; 27:12), we all need guidance and accountability. As parents, how do we live out the responsibility to bring up our children 'in the discipline and instruction of the Lord' (Eph. 6:4)?

Before we turn to principles of parental discipline, notice in this regard that the primary responsibility for disciplining children rests with *fathers* as the spiritual leaders in the home who are primarily responsible for the spiritual condition of the family before God (though mothers are paramount in implementing and should be centrally involved working in tandem with their husband). The following three major New Testament passages on this subject all directly and explicitly address fathers or represent them as primary agents of discipline:

- '*Fathers*, don't provoke your children to anger, but bring them up in the discipline and instruction of the Lord.' (Eph. 6:4)

- '*Fathers*, don't provoke your children, lest they become discouraged.' (Col. 3:21)

- 'It is for discipline that you have to endure. God is treating you as sons. For what son is there whom his *father* does not discipline? … We have had earthly *fathers* who disciplined us and we respected them. … they disciplined us for a short time as it seemed best to them. … Therefore, lift your drooping hands and strengthen your weak knees' (Heb. 12:7-11)

Therefore, fathers should be careful to live out their role as leaders in the enterprise of disciplining and directing their child's development. As you walk out the door and head out for work, you should not be delegating the discipline of the children to your wife *in toto*; you should rather plan, pray, and remain together in close partnership with your wife. Work out ways to keep in touch. Call her and call the children during the day to show you care and are involved. At the end of day, be responsible to check and encourage everyone in the journey toward Christlikeness!

While we're at it, notice also the helpful references to the different responses our children may have to fatherly discipline in the above-cited passages: They may respond in anger (Eph. 6:4), become discouraged (Col. 3:21), or be tempted to give up (Heb. 12:12-13). Our child's response may be signs we are overdoing it or approaching things incorrectly. Yet while discipline may seem painful and unpleasant at the time, Scripture tells us that the result will be holiness and righteousness in the lives of those who endure discipline and have been trained by it (Heb. 12:11, 14).

Finally, embrace the biblical scope of discipline as framed in the passages highlighted. The Greek term for discipline is *paideia*, which is broader than mere correction or punishment. Ephesians 6:4 speaks of 'discipline *and instruction.*' In 2 Timothy 3:16, Paul says Scripture's purpose is *'teaching*, rebuke, correction, and *training in righteousness.*' Thus, we shouldn't think of discipline merely or even primarily in *negative* terms, though it doubtless involves correction. More positively, it is setting a child on a straight path, equipping them in moral formation and shaping of their character, so they will be 'complete, equipped for every good work' (2 Tim. 3:17).

How, then, can we best help our children deal with their sinful nature and the temptations they face in and from the world around them? Not that we have the definitive answer on this issue, but here are seven useful insights regarding parental discipline adapted from my book *God, Marriage, and Family*. Discipline should be:

1. Consistent and predictable: It's *hard* to be consistent in discipline, with each individual personality, among different children, over many years of parenting. And yet consistency is *so* important, because it helps reinforce in our children a proper view of God and their sin and what godly conduct should look like in our lives—and it aids in making sure there are no surprises along the way!

It's helpful here to consider the biblical example of Eli, a spiritual leader in Israel, who didn't sufficiently or consistently guide his sons in the knowledge of the Lord or keep them accountable. As a result, his sons didn't believe in God or serve him (1 Sam. 2:23-25).

To keep parental discipline in proper balance, however, note the scriptural contrast made with the godly young Samuel following the description of Eli's wayward sons. Samuel, who likely had little parental discipline to shape him, was soon 'growing in stature and in favor both with the LORD and with men' (1 Sam. 2:26 NASB; cf. 1:11, 26-28), having been dedicated to the Lord. God works here in ways beyond our comprehension, as in the case of Hannah, a formerly barren woman, who committed her child to the Lord for His purposes, realizing this child was not her own in the first place. Despite the fact that he grew up without parents to discipline and guide him, he became a true servant of God.

2. Age-appropriate: It may seem obvious, but while discipline should be consistent, the form of discipline will likely change depending on the age of the child or young person. While you may choose to physically discipline a small child (in love, not anger), or use time-out or loss of privilege for children a little older yet still young, parenting older children will typically involve more reasoning and interaction (though loss of privilege will still be appropriate—no new basketball shoes or no use of the family car!). The important lesson here is that while we need to encourage a mind-set of constant accountability and discipline, the way we exercise these will need to grow with and adapt to our children as they grow older.

3. Fair and just: The goal of discipline is not to punish the child! That's part of the process, but the greater purpose is to point the way forward toward restoration and godliness, helping them to be aware of their sin, and to keep them accountable for it. In entering a relational encounter of disciplining your child, try to keep the perspective of your role as a responsible steward of the Lord. Make certain that the 'punishment fits the crime.'

'But it isn't fair!' is a perennial favorite in many families when a child is disciplined. Perhaps there are times when we aren't consistent or have leveled a punishment that was too harsh. In any case, the craving for fairness is God-given and right, and we should try to be fair (though still merciful, because our God is very compassionate). Remember, our parental credibility is at stake: If we overreact at first and then reduce the punishment and do this often, our children won't take us seriously after a while. The Bible repeatedly tells parents not to be too harsh with their children or to discourage or exasperate them (Eph. 6:4; Col. 3:21). Remember too that we should have no favorites, or even be open to the charge of favoritism.

4. Child-specific: At the same time, it is equally true that when it comes to discipline, what may work with one child may not work equally well with another. This is because God made each child unique. Some children are more sensitive to discipline while others are more intransigent. Some are more compliant while others tend to be more independently-minded. Parental wisdom is required in balancing the need for fairness with the need for child-specific discipline that will be most effective in achieving the desired purpose. Our goals include setting proper boundaries, developing character, and teaching children that there are consequences for their actions.

5. Administered in love, not anger: It goes without saying that discipline should be administered in love, not anger. Of course, this is easier said than done, especially when frustration and resentment have built up over time. Keep in mind that when your child disobeys you, the ultimate problem isn't so much that you've been affronted but that God has been disregarded and offended. Our goal in parenting is to be an instrument in bringing our children under the authority of God. Parenting is a sacred trust and stewardship. Any offense to you—the parent—is minor compared to the responsibility that is ours to guide them to love and respect God.

There are times when we may discipline our child in anger and need to apologize to them later. We've found that it helps if one of us has any resentment, or anger, we do our best to let the other handle the situation. If you're by yourself (spouse at work or out or you're a single parent) you can always ask your child to cool down in their room for ten-fifteen minutes to give a chance for you to calm down first before addressing unruly behavior. It doesn't help to complicate matters by detracting attention from the actual problem because a parent is unable to handle their own irritations.

6. Forward-looking: In administering discipline, we don't want to be past-oriented (What just happened?), because we can't change the past. We don't want to be stuck in the present (Will our child ever learn? What have I done wrong as a parent?). Rather, we should adopt a forward-looking point of view which focuses on our children's growth in character and on God's work in their lives and learning to parent according to this end (Prov. 22:6; Heb. 12:11). Our hope is not found in self-effort but in spiritual transformation through God's Word and His Holy Spirit both in our lives and in the children. Seen in that light, any one small infraction is not that big a deal in and of itself but can serve as an occasion to teach our children vital lessons about life and their relationship with God and others.

7. Part of the parent-child relationship: This last point may be the most important in the context of the type of realistic, relational, and responsible approach to parenting that we advocate in this book. Discipline is part of our *relationship* with our child. Our children are works in progress, they are human beings who struggle with sin and selfishness and insecurity just like we still do. We should not condemn them; they desperately need our help and understanding and partnership in this delicate, delightful venture of growing up to become a man or woman of God. What a privilege it is to be a part of God's work in the life of another precious human being—the children with whom He has entrusted us.

Principles of Parental Discipline

	Principle of Parental Discipline	Explanation/Rationale
1	Consistent and predictable	Same offense, same punishment; know what punishment is
2	Age-appropriate	Will look different for elementary school child than teenager
3	Fair and just	Punishment fit the 'crime'; not too harsh
4	Child-specific	Tailored to personality of individual child

	Principle of Parental Discipline	Explanation/Rationale
5	Administered in love, not anger	Avoid annoyed or unduly personal reaction, convey a sense of love
6	Forward-looking	Not focused on past offense or current crisis but on desired result
7	Part of the parent-child relationship	Respect and dignity as part of relational parenting approach

Practical Application

So how do we practically recognize and live out our parenting responsibilities in view of these principles? As you begin to go about your days with your children, offer your children and your service as a parent to God. Submit yourself to all that He has for your children, and to the role you have in their lives. Always be prayerful. Recognize your own limitations, and the stewardship from God that parenting represents. Focus on an approach to your children that will encourage spiritual flourishing and realize that parenting is more of a ministry than a task.

As the child grows and begins to display their personality and sin nature, in their own 'creative' ways, *be discerning* and *learn to recognize manipulation*. Be careful yourself, not to bribe them just to keep the peace. And be prepared to say 'no' when your child asks you to buy extra items in the grocery store checkout line and craves yet another item after you've just bought several. Be consistent in keeping determined boundaries. Feel free to let your child see your dependence on the Lord as you seek Him in parenting. You may even turn to God in spontaneous prayer at times when you need guidance, even out loud in the very presence of your infant, toddler, or older child. Remember: You'll help them not to become a self-centered, materialistic, always-want-more individual by these kinds of attitudes and boundaries. Model servanthood and sacrifice to them in your personal life and remind them verbally that their happiness doesn't depend on getting everything they want.

Talking to your child about their innate proclivity toward selfishness and sin may be the initial step that helps them realize their need for a savior. If they've trusted Christ already, such spiritual instruction, discussion, and guidance will help them learn to confess their sin and turn to Him for help as a way of life. Tell them and show them that you, too, are weak and vulnerable without Christ and that we all depend on Him to be delivered from ourselves so we can truly live for Him and for others.

Helping your child focus on others rather than themselves through sharing and giving an item such as a toy or favorite treat is a good start. Encourage them to do something for their sibling, even, or especially, if it involves sacrifice. When the opportunity arises, bring them along in your service at church, Bible studies, prayer meetings, and on service projects or mission trips. The younger child can be encouraged to serve in small yet helpful ways such as setting up chairs for a meeting or preparing food with you for a ministry group. As you do, articulate your reason for helping others and help them experience the joy of giving and serving people. As *you* serve the Lord from the heart, *they* can experience the overflow of your joy and fulfillment that inevitably comes. They can begin to experience the internal satisfaction for themselves in smaller and gradually greater ways as they grow spiritually and experientially serving God.

Conclusion

Your child is a sinner. Don't fight this notion in your parenting—accept it and address the root problem, not merely the symptoms. How can you do this? Good question. First, realize that there are forces greater than your child's will at work. Apart from conversion and spiritual regeneration, your child can't consistently obey you, and even *with* conversion there's a need for continual guidance. A parenting approach that focuses merely on external behavior regulation and modification will prove inadequate. We begin by stirring our child's awareness that he or she is a sinner who needs a savior, the Lord Jesus Christ.

Only true, heartfelt repentance and trust in Christ will enable your child to receive the Holy Spirit who will take up residence in him or her. In the Spirit's power, your child will be able not merely to conform to your expectations externally but to render genuine obedience. This, incidentally, is the same kind of relationship God desires to have with all his children, including you and me. In this way, as we've seen in the previous chapter, the fatherhood of God serves as the model, the anchor, the paradigm of parenting that is grounded in the reality of life in this world, which regrettably but unalterably includes the reality of brokenness and sin.

♦ *What, if any, adjustments do you need to make in your view of your children in view of reading this chapter? Have you been too optimistic, too pessimistic, or accurate about their innate proclivity toward sin?*

♦ *How does the realization of your child's thoroughgoing sinfulness affect your understanding of your role as parent? Do you need to adjust your expectations or your approach toward your children in any way, and if so, how?*

♦ *What can you do to implement parenting discipline techniques as described in this chapter with the goal of changing hearts rather than simply enforcing outward conformity through punishment?*

3
The World

Parenting is a privilege with which God entrusts us. At the same time, it takes place in an imperfect world, within a complex web of ungodly values, in the face of indwelling sin, and in the presence of potential attacks by the devil. As you begin this chapter, reflect on the following passages to come to terms with these realities in parenting.

♦ *Read 1 John 2:15-17. How can this passage be applied to the challenge and opportunity of parenting children in the world in which we live? Give specific examples.*

♦ *Read Proverbs 3:5-6. Reflect on this passage's relevance to your own life, then ask how this passage also relates to your role as a parent, and to your children's lives as well.*

'I'm overwhelmed!' All of us have felt that way, let's be real. Not only do we as parents need to be realistic about our own role in parenting and our child's sinful nature, we also need to be realistic about the imperfect world in which all parenting of necessity takes place. This isn't a perfect world—not even close—though evidence of God's reality and presence abounds everywhere. So, if, as a mom or dad, you feel overwhelmed in the face of the challenge of raising a child that loves God and pursues His purpose for his or her life, be encouraged that part of the reason why parenting can be challenging in this world is because the world itself isn't always a friendly, conducive place for parenting.

In fact, contrary to idealistic notions of parenting, raising children takes place in the context of real life, continual stress, and this imperfect world. It took us a while to realize this, but often the problem—if there is a problem—is not lack of parenting skills or spiritual immaturity (or a myriad of other options), but somewhat trivial factors at the intersection of fallenness and finitude, like stress, busyness, or fatigue.

To cope with the pressures of life and parenting, parents need regular rest and refreshment. They need encouragement in relationships, instruction and mentoring, prayer, and community support. They will also benefit from practicing fiscal responsibility, dealing with their finances with care and integrity. Learning to make sensible, daily, lifestyle choices is also important in the messy and sometimes mundane life we live. Moreover, parents have a need to be sexually fulfilled, a vital reality of wholesome living in this physical and material world. So, before we move into the relational dimension of parenting, let's take some time to address all these imperative issues.

The World, the Flesh, and the Devil

The Bible teaches that there are three major enemies that will be continually confronting anyone who wants to serve God and live for Him. These are the *world*, the *flesh*, and the *devil*. To make matters worse, these enemies aren't unrelated but rather closely interconnected. At the fall of humanity, the devil tempted the woman, and she succumbed to the temptation, and thus, the devil's reasoning and rebellion entered the woman's nature and the man's as well. Now human culture—the world system and its values and desires—has a self-centered, God-resistant bent, and the devil is the 'Ruler of this world' (John 12:31; 14:30; 1 John 5:19).

Parenting and Culture

The relationship between Christians and culture is a tricky one. On the one hand are those who demonize culture, claiming that culture itself is demonic. If so, believers must have nothing to do with it and be always separate. Others say—or at least act like they believe—that culture is essentially good, or at least neutral, so that Christians can freely participate in the culture. Then there are many positions between these two poles that to varying degrees advocate a discerning, cautious participation in the culture, so that Christians can maintain witness without compromise. The biblical call is for spiritual—but not physical—separation from the fallen world system. As Jesus put it, believers are in the world but 'not of the world' (John 17). Paul asserted that 'our citizenship is in heaven' (Phil. 3:20) and Peter called us 'resident aliens' (1 Pet. 1:1; 2:11).

It's of course helpful to realize that the world's values are diametrically opposed to those of Christ. Its goals, priorities, and standards are much different from those Jesus exhibited during His time on earth. The apostle Paul makes this clear when he writes, 'I appeal to you therefore, brothers, by the mercies of God, to present your bodies as a living sacrifice, holy and acceptable to God, which is your spiritual worship. Do not be conformed to this world, but be transformed by the renewal of your mind, that by testing you may discern what is the will of God, what is good and acceptable and perfect' (Rom. 12:1-2).

What God desires from us is not *assimilation* or *accommodation* to the culture but *transformation*. As Christians, we should seek to be transformed rather than conform to the thinking of this world. This involves a renewal of our minds. We ought to think differently, and then we should act differently, because we're driven by different beliefs about life in this world. Life is not about self; it's about loving and serving God and others. When Jesus was asked about God's expectations for His people, he responded in this way: 'You shall love the Lord your God with all your heart and with all your soul and with all your mind. This is the great and first commandment. And a second is like it: You shall love your neighbor as yourself' (Matt. 22:37-39).

Do you and I always love God with all our heart, soul, and mind? Of course not. But this is what we should do, and this is what God expects. As believers, of course, we have the indwelling Holy Spirit to help us live in this thoroughly supernatural way. Jesus said many other amazing things about the way citizens of His kingdom should live.

Many of these are found in the Sermon on the Mount (Matt. 5–7). We should love rather than hate our enemies (Matt. 5:44); we should pray that God's kingdom—not ours—be advanced on this earth; we should act toward others as we would want them to act toward us (Matt. 7:12); we shouldn't worry about earthly concerns or possessions because God will supply all our needs; and so on (Matt. 5:48; 6:9-11, 33-34). This is the new ethic for the citizens of the kingdom. Would you agree that this ethic is radically different from the values, desires, and priorities of the culture in which we live?

And yet, God so loved the world that He gave His one and only Son to die for us on the cross (John 3:16). This doesn't mean that He indulged in sin, of course, or that He acceded to the world's values out of peer pressure or a desire to be popular. Not at all. God was willing, in Jesus Christ, to enter this world which rejected, hated, and persecuted Him and to act redemptively toward sinful humanity. No doubt about it, Jesus told His followers, the world will hate you; it will hate you because you're not one of them and because you won't go along with its pressure to conform to its values (John 15:18-20; 16:1-2). You must be willing to suffer with me and, if necessary, even die for your faith.

In one sense, then, we *should* love the world. Like Jesus, we should be set apart for God's service and then live in this world so people can see that we're different because of His work in our lives (John 17:17-19).

One thing we've found instructive as we've studied the life of Jesus in the Gospels over the years is our Lord's example. Jesus was no monk, recluse, or hermit. He didn't withdraw from the world and live in a monastery and devote Himself to prayer and fasting all His days. To be sure, He withdrew occasionally so He could spend extended times in prayer and prepare to go back into the world that hated and yet needed Him so desperately. In fact, Jesus was so compassionate and merciful that people gave Him the epithet 'friend of … sinners' (Matt. 11:19). The Pharisees who stuck that label on Him didn't mean it as a compliment, mind you, but as a pejorative term. They, the 'Separate Ones,' practiced their righteousness ostentatiously, priding themselves on treating 'sinners' with contempt—but not Jesus.

Raising Culturally Astute Christian Children

What kind of Christian are you? And what kind of Christians do you intend to raise in your children? That's a huge challenge, but it's a matter you'll want to think through carefully and discuss together as a couple. Most importantly, the decision starts with you, long before you teach your children. If you're dealing with this issue for the first time when you discover your son is addicted to pornography or your teenage daughter is pregnant, you've probably been too busy to give this important matter the attention it deserves.

We believe that we should be thoughtful and theologically grounded in thinking about our God-intended relationship with the world and the surrounding culture rather than merely making *ad hoc* decisions based on the circumstances or people involved. Two people can watch a given movie for very different reasons. One may watch it for self-gratification while another may do so to establish common ground with their friends so they can be salt and light and talk to them about their faith in gracious conversation. The same thing is true if you choose to go to a bar or engage in any number of activities.

At the Fall, the narrative tells us the following about the reasoning process that led the woman to disobey God's command: 'So when the woman saw that the tree was good for food, and that it was a delight to the eyes, and that the tree was to be desired to make one wise, she took of its fruit and ate …' (Gen. 3:6). So, we see that the woman rationalized living for self rather than for God by reasoning that the fruit she contemplated eating was delicious—it appealed to her senses—that it was attractive and appealing to look at, and that it would advance her knowledge.

People have reasoned in a comparable manner ever since. The apostle John may have had this story in mind when he wrote, 'Do not love the world or the things in the world. If anyone loves the world, the love of the Father is not in him. For all that is in the world—the desires of the flesh and the desires of the eyes and pride of life—is not from the Father but is from the world. And the world is passing away along with its desires, but whoever does the will of God abides forever' (1 John 2:15-17).

We started out this chapter by thinking about the three major enemies with which we must contend while living on this earth: the world, the flesh, and the devil. The devil will tap into the values of this fallen world to appeal to your flesh and to that of your son and daughter. Unless they're grounded in biblical truth, this can be a deadly combination. Christian parenting in this world is deeply countercultural and involves taking a stance that is rooted firmly in God's Word rather than being grounded in our culture and the world around us.

Busyness, Fatigue, and Need for Rest

This is an imperfect world, and we're human. That means, among other things, that we're limited and finite—we get tired and our capacity to handle stress is not boundless. When it comes to parenting, this means that we can take only so much before we become cranky or lose our temper, or merely lack energy. A wise parent, therefore, will recognize their limitations and plan times for refreshment and relaxation to recharge batteries and to reconnect with God and with their spouse at a deeper level.

When we started our marriage and parenting journey, I read James Dobson's *What Wives Wish Husbands Knew about Women*. One thing I still remember about reading this book many years ago, is Dr Dobson pointing out that the greatest challenge with which wives struggle in their marriage and in parenting is *fatigue*. I remember thinking: What—fatigue, the biggest problem in marriage? That's certainly not what I expected to hear. I'm sure many other men felt the same. But when I went to my wife and asked her what she thought, she heartily agreed.

So, husbands, if you're on the front end of the journey, please realize that you've got to have a plan for when your wife feels overwhelmed or tired. Come alongside her to help her, order a takeout for dinner, get a babysitter and take her out on a date or if possible, take a day off during the week and give her a break, so she can read the Bible leisurely, go to a tearoom with a friend, or get away from the continual demands of household chores and beloved, yet taxing children.

In the busyness of our days, it's easy to find ourselves operating in maintenance mode. Every day we get up, get ready for the day, eat breakfast, and then go to work, or start school or take our children to school, and throughout the day do the things that call for our attention. The next day, we do the same, and so weeks, and months, and even years, go by. Gradually couples begin to accumulate stuff. Eventually they run out of space. Some begin to fill a storage unit or may move to a bigger house. We've learned that, in view of this tendency, it's helpful to keep things simple, embracing a type of 'holy minimalism,' regularly cleaning house and sharing the wealth of gathered things—or getting rid of them.

There are certainly more important things in life than advancing one's career and chasing the things that our flesh craves for gratification, comfort, expediency, and even self-aggrandizement. Have you made the decision to put God and your family first in this regard? If so, you've laid the foundation for setting a powerful example for your children, and more likely than not, they'll do the same. An undue focus on things can seriously distract us from a fruitful life of service to God and effective parenting, but just as counterproductive may be a life of hyperactive, frenetic busyness (as much as some of us might think that this enables us to do more for God or for His kingdom sometimes).

In fact, busyness doesn't mean we're diligent, faithful, or fruitful. A full schedule doesn't necessarily mean that we're in the center of God's will or accomplishing the things God wants us to do. Doing everything people ask us to do, everything we want to do, and most everything that comes our way and isn't sinful or immoral demonstrates a need for screening devices in our lives, called 'wisdom' and 'discernment.' Examining all the opportunities presented and filtering them through the lens of what we understand God's calling on our lives to be is crucial for a life lived to the glory of God.

We lived in the same locale for the majority of our children's childhood years. This has provided a stable environment for our children, which has enabled them to go to be schooled, grow and develop, and go to college, being anchored in a family and a place that is home. In this age of transience and fast-paced technological development, this experience of permanence and rootedness is increasingly rare, yet is something to be treasured.

The reality is, this is where people live. We're doing too much, moving too often, and have too little time for the most important responsibility: our children. As parents, we can easily get overcommitted if we're not careful. Our children, too, can get so busy with various activities—all good and unobjectionable in and of themselves—that there remains little time for reflection, rest, and quality time. Most importantly, their time with the Lord can easily get squeezed out or even vanish into non-existence. Nothing is worth such a hectic lifestyle. A busy life may flatter our egos and serve as a sort of escape mechanism—no need to come to terms with our loneliness, unanswered questions, uncertainty regarding our calling, our future spouse, and so forth—but it hardly ever permanently and successfully serves as a substitute for doing a few things well. Be still and know your God and listen to Him (Ps. 46:10). Take time out amid the relentless clamor of life. Stop and look around. And take notice of what God is doing in your life and in the lives of your children.

Resolve to do a few things well—your relationship with God, time with one another and with family, and serving God in your local church with an intelligent, meaningful, and strategic focus. Take some time at your earliest convenience and ask yourself the question: Am I doing too much? Am I able to do everything that I'm currently doing with excellence? Or am I in perennial rush and maintenance mode? If so, maybe it's time for you to divest yourself of certain responsibilities and to step aside for someone else to give himself fully to that task that you're able to do only half-heartedly. What's more, resolve to model a quality lifestyle in front of your children and to encourage them to screen opportunities that come their way.

Finally, there's no substitute for the trusty old To-Do list to help us stay balanced and keep the task of parenting central in our lives. If it's on that list, it'll get done! These indicate my priorities, though nothing is too small to be put on that list. By putting even small items on that list, I keep my mind free from unnecessary clutter which allows me to focus on bigger priorities throughout the day and the week. The Bible says, 'Commit your work to the LORD, and your plans will be established' (Prov. 16:3). It also says, 'Commit your way to the LORD; trust in him, and he will act.... Be still before the LORD and wait patiently for him' (Ps. 37:5, 7). Let God screen your tasks and your daily life and ask Him when you face major decisions. Your life is an open book before Him. Cultivate the lost art of waiting for *Him*, and *He* will direct your paths (Prov. 3:5-6).

Need for Encouragement, Support, and Mentoring

We've talked about the need for occasional times of rest and refreshment. By this we're not thinking merely of the yearly summer vacation (though that's important, too, and many lifelong memories are formed there). We're also talking about more frequent and regular ways which enable us to cope with the considerable demands on our time and energy as parents. Living at a considerable distance from our parents, we personally have not had family nearby to support us through our years of parenting (though the children have enjoyed seeing their grandparents on special trips). Instead, we've craved and benefited from other kinds of support, whether through our local church community or friends.

My wife will tell you that it's been hard not having more support, and there's only so much a husband can do, even though a supportive husband is certainly something every wife and mother will desire very deeply. In any case, if you're a young couple, be grateful for family support (of course, we realize there can be challenges there, too, as in-laws may not always share the same values as we do). Husbands, recognize your wife's need for tangible support and encouragement. The Bible tells us husbands to be considerate toward our wives as the 'weaker vessel' and to treat them as fellow heirs of grace (1 Pet. 3:7). Our wives depend on us and on our understanding and active undergirding.

Our partnership as parents is vital. Partnership means we tackle the task of parenting *together*, as a *team*. By 'partnership' we don't mean delegation where the husband passes on to his wife the responsibility of caring for the children during the day, and in some cases schooling them at home, while he remains largely disengaged and disconnected. Staying in close contact during the day and empathizing with one another will go a *long* way to make the challenges that are sure to come more bearable and to help you emerge even stronger and victorious in the end.

I, Margaret, have long realized the importance of mentoring. I love the passage in the book of Titus where older, more mature women are encouraged to teach young women to love their husbands and children, to manage their household well, and to cultivate godly Christian virtues and character traits as women (Titus 2:3-5). It clearly indicates that there is a need in the lives of young women for training in marriage and motherhood. However, more mature women are often too busy to reach out to young women in the church (especially those from a non-Christian background). If you're reading this and you are a mature Christian woman, make room in your life for mentoring one or several young women in your church. This is a vital ministry—to pass on what you've learned in years of marriage and parenting to the next generation.

The Big Three: Sex, Money, and In-Laws

Perhaps the three areas that are the trickiest to navigate in marriage with palpable implications for parenting are sex, money, and in-laws. Young parents often seem to be ill-equipped to handle financial matters. Popular shows regularly convey the notion that married people don't have sex. In-laws are nearly always portrayed negatively. Two families merging together may create tension, friction, and a clash of conflicting values. Compromised sexual history and background may contribute to the stress and conflict a couple may experience, and it probably will take a while for each to learn how to relate to the other in this vital area. Regarding finances, each spouse may be accustomed to different standards of living and spending habits. Parenting—particularly, having a baby—amid these various kinds of adjustments and stressors will likely be rendered even more challenging. Fortunately, helpful resources on all these topics are readily available. Nevertheless, let's talk for a minute about each of these potential sources of strain on marriage and family.

In-laws and Family Traditions

You may remember the old saying, 'Women: can't live with them, can't live without them.' Yes, marriage, and the merging of two different people itself is a challenge. This statement, applied to *in-laws*, though, works well too, as two different families merge. The Bible says that when a man gets married, he *leaves* his father and mother and is united to his wife (Gen. 2:24). Not only does this reflect God's arrangement, these are also very wise words. While both of you owe a lot to your families of origin, and love your parents deeply, it'll be vital to understand that you've started (or are about to start) a family of your own. This is a new venture for you, no matter how good the role models might have been in your families, and you'll need some space to do so.

You'll need to talk at some length about forming your own family traditions or maybe adapting ones you grew up with—things as simple (or complicated) as belief in Santa Claus. (We chose to largely refrain from participating in activities related to Santa Claus.) What about Halloween? (We'll let you figure that one out for yourself.) More importantly, you'll need to decide how you want to raise your children, with the wise guidance of your parents, yet without their *undue* interference.

At the same time, this doesn't mean you should shut your parents out of your parenting. To the contrary, you may want to ask for input and advice (remember, you don't have to take the advice if you disagree). If you are an older parent, it'll be wise to allow our newlywed children, or those preparing for marriage, some space. You may find them approaching you more readily to talk about relationships, career choices, important decisions, and other issues.

Practicing Fiscal Responsibility

Moving on to the second of the 'Big Three,' then, we come to *money*. The Bible says to avoid the love of money (1 Tim. 6:10)—i.e., greed—but money itself is something we all need so we can pay our bills and support our families. Speaking of paying bills, did you know that money—along with in-laws and sex—is one of the biggest sources of conflict in marriage? It seems there's never enough of it, which is why we should try to distinguish between needs and wants. Often what becomes a source of contention is an expensive hobby or habit, whether the husband's leisure pursuit or women's love of nice clothing (though, of course, as husbands we want our wives to look beautiful, and wives want their husbands to have some outlet and opportunity to relax). Make sure that you're accountable to each other in this regard, even if the problem is not a gambling habit or something more serious that may require professional help.

It'll often be one or the other who is more capable of doing the finances. As a couple, we try to confer with each other especially in the case of bigger purchases, and even shopping patterns (such as where we normally go to buy groceries). Over time, those kinds of things add up to significant amounts. We have a general budget of how much we can spend. We pay federal and local taxes. We have a plan for saving for our children's college education. We also have a car fund and a rainy-day fund. We have a retirement fund. In all of this, we trust God to provide for our needs and look to Him for wisdom and guidance. We also try to give to our local church as well as support various individuals and couples or families on the mission field, whether nationally or internationally.

When it comes to parenting, finances are important, too. On a general scale, it's our lifestyle choices—avoiding debt, being content with a smaller house, having only one car—that will set a baseline for our children as they move on to establish their own patterns of consumption. These will be our children's expectations that will need to be articulated and managed as they meet that special person with whom they explore marriage. Another crucial area is credit card bills and debt. We've always had just one credit card and paid it off monthly. We've also tried to pay for our purchases up front (even for cars), though we did take out a small loan when we bought our family van and had to take out a mortgage when we purchased our house.

Teaching our children about the importance of saving and delayed gratification and cautioning them against incurring excessive debt are critical issues in parenting. By this we can protect our children from sliding into financial bondage. Personally, we place a high value on our children's education as a strategic investment in their future. For this reason we've allotted significant funds to paying for college and have told our children that we don't want finances to be a major factor when it comes to choosing college (within reason). In terms of delayed gratification and fiscal responsibility, we loaned our second car to our children (which they shared, took to college, and passed down) rather than buying them a car of their own. This was helpful not only in saving money but also in setting an example of frugality.

While we're talking about money, teach your children honesty in financial matters. This is one of the principal areas where we should exercise integrity. We should pay what we owe. We should understand the concept of *stewardship*—that we're ultimately managing money for God and are called to be a blessing to others. Help your children be grateful for the ways in which God provides for their and their family's needs and help them see how you're trusting God to provide. Help them also learn how to live within their means and to be frugal regarding discretionary expenses on entertainment, eating out, vacations, etc.

Another set of ideas pertains to creative dates and leisure activities for parents and families. We love going for hikes, bike rides, and the occasional trip to a museum. Our local art museum hosts outdoor movie nights once a week in the summer, which is a terrific way of watching a recent (or decent) film together, plus enjoying a picnic before the show gets underway. A little while ago, we added a basketball court and a fire pit adjacent to our house. These additions have given our children and family hours of safe and healthy activity, plus have made our house a much more attractive destination for visitors, including our children's friends and families we know. You get the picture—there are ways to have fun that are healthier and often less costly if we take the time to be thoughtful and strategic when it comes to family outings and leisure activities, whether for us as couples or with the entire family.

Sex and Parenting

We'll close this chapter with a few words about *sex*. We're not talking here about sex in marriage in general but marital sex in relation to parenting. Lack of sexual fulfillment can cause a lot of frustration and become the source of significant conflict. Husbands, realize that faithfulness to your wife is a matter of your heart (Matt. 5:27-28), not merely staying in the marriage while finding part of your sexual gratification elsewhere, whether in other relationships or in virtual substitutes. Wives, please realize that sex may be more important to your husbands than you realize, and to yourself possibly, too. Therefore, try not to withhold sex as a means of manipulating your spouse (1 Cor. 7:3-5). Fulfillment in your sexual relationship is a vital part of your union and unity as a couple and as parents. In this way, you can partner in complementing each other as mom and dad to your children. And don't be afraid to show occasional affection toward each other in front of your children. They'll be happy to see their parents have a good relationship and really love each other.

One more thing: Wives, don't be too preoccupied with your children when spending time with your husband. It may be easier for us men to compartmentalize between parenting and having sex, but as much as possible, once parenting issues have been dealt with for the time being, it'll be important for the wife to put the children aside to focus on being with her husband—that's part of setting appropriate boundaries. At the same time, husbands, realize that it'll be hard for your wife to be intimate with you if there are unresolved issues that she's still working through in her mind. Also, sometimes it'll be hard to find time for sex if the children are around 24/7 and don't go to bed until 10 o'clock at night or even later. You'll have to train your children to accept that there'll be times when the bedroom door is locked. That'll teach them that mom and dad have a relationship, too, and that they should respect your privacy.

The lesson to be learned is this: We must set proper priorities in our lives, and marriage and family must be a key priority. All of us want to think that we've got our priorities straight, but do we? Does your spouse feel he or she has your undivided attention—ever? Or are you habitually distracted or preoccupied with work responsibilities or worries about the children or aging parents or a litany of other concerns? Let's commit our cares to God, and set proper boundaries, and then cherish and celebrate the good gifts He's given us in our life partner and our family. As the wise Preacher wrote many years ago, 'Enjoy life with the wife whom you love, all the days of your vain life that he has given you under the sun' (Eccles. 9:9).

Conclusion

Kiss perfect, idealistic parenting goodbye. Say hello to parenting in an imperfect world. Be realistic. Parenting is not just about parents and children; it's also about the imperfect world we live in. This world has many challenges that make parenting, with all our ideals, dreams, and expectations, a lot harder than it might otherwise be. First, there are the world, the flesh, and the devil, steadfastly seeking to undo what we try to instill in our children, causing us and them to stumble and fall, and succumb to various kinds of temptation.

Then, because we're human and finite, there are natural limitations such as lack of energy, fatigue, and need of rest—limitations we need to recognize and anticipate if we don't want to be a cranky, frantic, maxed-out parent who is way too busy to realize that he has turned into a rather unpleasant person to live with. Parents generally don't lack in good intentions; it's just that because of the stress and demands life throws at them they often aren't able to make good on those intentions as life gradually gets busier and busier.

This is also true regarding the 'Big Three'—sex, money, and in-laws. Again, a realistic approach to parenting will recognize that challenges will come in these areas and will try to be proactive and sensible in these pressure points of life.

♦ *What do you find to be the greatest successes and challenges in parenting? Are these internal obstacles (such as selfishness or fatigue) or external obstacles (such as financial pressures or spiritual warfare) or both? How do these challenges affect your parenting?*

♦ *Make a list of the people on whom you can call to support you as parents, such as your parents or in-laws, friends, people at church, or others (including babysitters). Do you have sufficient help or do you need to strengthen your network of support?*

♦ *Discuss any sources of frequent conflict, such as your relationship with your in-laws, financial matters, or your sexual relationship. What stresses are you facing? What can you do to improve? List specific steps and plan to implement them.*

Part 2
RELATIONAL PARENTING

Child and God, Child and Parent, Child and Others

Parenting takes place in the context of three sets of very important relationships: the child and God, the child and the parent, and the child with others (siblings, friends, church, etc.). We all need meaningful relationships and a social network of people who love us and care for us. God created us for community! The primary place where we find love and acceptance, apart from God, is usually our family. No one knows us better than our family, and if you're a young man or woman, you realize that no one typically *loves* you more than your parents. Yes, it's true! For this reason, it's vital that parents make *loving* their children a central plank in their approach to parenting. In one sense, to even say this seems redundant because virtually all parents *have* love for their children but this involves not only *telling* them that we love them but *showing* them that we do. At times our actual practice may fall short of our best intentions.

The second major tension you'll encounter in parenting then, is between cultivating the various important *relationships* in a child's life and that of following the *'rules'* of parenting (methods or techniques, etc.). Many parents approach parenting primarily as a task to be accomplished. If they follow certain steps, they will succeed. The problem is, children are a lot more complex than that! There's simply no magic formula, or series of steps, that by itself will guarantee success as a parent. In any case, how do you define success when it comes to parenting? In this portion of our book, we'll propose that parenting is essentially relational, and as parents we should put a priority on encouraging our children's relationship with God, cultivating our relationship with our children, and equipping them to deal effectively with conflict in the real world which is sure to come.

Conceiving of parenting at its root as a relationship is especially important as our children are older. The rules of the game change as they mature and can be more responsive to our rationale and reasoning. Many of us find that it's easier simply to keep everything under control and to make sure our children are taken care of, rather than to *spend time* with them. Parenting is *very* time-consuming! If you plan to do parenting 'on the clock,' as it were, chances are your relationship with your children won't be as deep as it could be. More than anything then, parenting is *presence.* As one person once remarked, 'Ninety percent of life is just showing up.' Apply this to parenting. Are you going to show up and be counted as a parent? Or are you going to parent by remote control, by keeping your children happy or by giving them things whenever they demand?

Chances are, you're in it for the long haul if you're reading this book. That's great! Our relationships with our children can be wonderfully rewarding if we pursue a *relationship* with them rather than keeping them at arm's length. What does that look like? First, dads, it means that we will be careful not to compartmentalize. We need to care more for our family and less about our career. Women will have an easier time with this, as most seem to be already hardwired for relationship. In fact, most of what I know about being a relational parent I learned from my wife.

4

Child and God

It's so important for parents to take responsibility to introduce their children to Christ. Only when a child trusts Christ will they be able to glorify God and enjoy Him forever, living out their primary destiny. All their relationships with others, including parents, will spring from a transformed and renewed heart. And the Holy Spirit will become a powerful ally in spiritual transformation and begin to shape character. As you read the passages below, reflect on how God may be at work in your child's life.

> ◆ *Read 2 Peter 1:3-11. How do you balance grace and effort in the Christian life, and how do you encourage the same balance in the lives of your children?*
>
> ◆ *Read 1 Timothy 4:12. How can you encourage your children to develop Christian virtues and grow in character and integrity even in their younger years?*

As important as it is to practice relational parenting and to develop a close relationship with your child, the horizontal relationships of *family* should never be the ultimate level of parenting. The core of parenting should rather revolve around introducing your child to *God* in *Christ* and shepherding their growth in Christ (encouraging the vertical relationship of your child's relationship with his creator). God has given you, the parent, a role to be used as His *instrument* in your child's life.

Toward that end, we can instruct, set the example, and inspire our children. The overflow of our relationship with Christ will be evident as we live it out before them and pour our lives into them. A primary goal, then, is to be a part of leading our child toward a relationship with God; first by introducing them to their savior. This involves teaching our child about their innate sinfulness and need for repentance and faith in Jesus Christ.

That said, you can't put God in a box. If He so chooses, He'll open your child's mind to spiritual realities anytime, anywhere, whichever way He sees fit. One of our children received Christ while on a break during church. He was barely four years old, and he and I were in worship. He told me he needed to leave (for a restroom break), so I went with him. While there, he took the opportunity to ask me a spiritual question. One thing led to another, and by the time we left the bathroom, I had led him to a saving knowledge of Christ! Of course, the conversation didn't pop up in a vacuum (and the church service probably stirred his thinking); we had talked about the gospel before and there have been many spiritual conversations since then. In any case, for the Christian parent there certainly is no greater joy than seeing your child come to Christ and then grow in Him.

When your children trust in Christ for salvation, the Holy Spirit will enter their life and work from within to begin to transform them into ever-greater conformity to the character of Christ. It is key to understand that all our instructions are merely external to the child, and that without Christ they lack the inner capacity and power to consistently obey them. But the Spirit can do His work within them after salvation. He can convict them of their sin and give them both the desire and the ability to do what's right. As Paul writes, 'Work out your own salvation with fear and trembling, for it is God who works in you, both to will and to work for his good pleasure' (Phil. 2:12-13).

As a parent, this is what we want to see in our children: not merely external compliance, but inner transformation. In this regard, the Spirit is our all-important source and ally. The prophet Jeremiah envisioned the new covenant which would inaugurate the 'age of the Spirit' characterized by such inner transformation: 'For this is the covenant that I will make with the house of Israel after those days, declares the LORD: I will put my law within them, and I will write it on their hearts. And I will be their God, and they shall be my people' (Jer. 31:33).

What makes your child a Christian is *not* being born of Christian parents, growing up in a Christian family, or going to church. Until they repent of their sin and place their trust in the finished cross-work of Christ for themselves, their heart remains unregenerate and their sinful nature holds them in bondage to act on the prompting of their sinful nature.

A Gospel Conversation

As you talk to your child, here is what you'll want to make sure you address:

1. **Does he understand that he is a sinner?** Or does he think he occasionally does the wrong thing but is basically OK? If so, explain that the reason why he does wrong things is because he is a sinner. In that sense, he is *not* OK. Something is wrong with him (as with everyone) deep down inside; it's called his 'sinful nature.' Pray that God will give him a sense of his own sinfulness, which will prepare him to understand his need for salvation.

2. **Does he understand what Jesus did for him on the cross?** Or is he as I (Andreas) was growing up—totally mystified as to why Jesus was pictured hanging on a cross (even though I grew up in a nominal Roman Catholic home)? Explain to him that God, in His love, sent His only Son, the Lord Jesus, to die for him on the cross, as his sinless substitute, bearing the punishment he deserved, so he can be reconciled to God and live in relationship with Him the way God intends him to. Stir in him a desire to know God intimately and directly; this can happen only if he repents and places his trust in Christ.

3. **Does he understand what he needs to do to become a Christian?** Or is he fuzzy about this? Does he think this is something his parents can do for him? Or does he think he simply needs to try harder to be good and stop doing wrong things? Explain to him the

wonderful concept of God's grace, in which salvation is a gift that is totally undeserved and cannot be earned. Explain that we need salvation but that God knew we can never save ourselves, so He sent Jesus to save us. All he is expected to do is gratefully accept God's gracious provision through repentance and faith. Praise God!

Of course, even if a person is converted, it's not the case that once the Spirit comes to live within them, they no longer sin. Far from it. They're spiritual infants whose relationship with the Lord must be gently and consistently nourished. As Peter writes, 'since you have been born again, not of perishable seed but of imperishable, through the living and abiding word of God ... Like newborn infants, long for the pure spiritual milk, that by it you may grow up into salvation—if indeed you have tasted that the Lord is good' (1 Pet. 1:23; 2:2-3).

If your child is a genuine child of God, there'll be hunger for reading the Bible and praying, though their sinful nature and impulses will fight against this, just as in our own lives as believers. There may be times when your child may be less responsive to the Spirit and when there's spiritual dryness. There also may be times when we unfortunately shut them down by not allowing room for the expression of the Spirit in their lives. So, be intentional in encouraging them to read the Bible and letting the Word of God do its work in their hearts and minds. And pray! When they're old enough, you can get them a good Study Bible and show them how to consult the footnotes if they have a question about a passage in the text. Educate yourself biblically, so that you'll be able to engage their spiritual questions as they arise. You never know when they may come. Also, model and encourage them to be real in prayer—moving beyond set, formulaic prayers—and to pray not only for themselves and their family but for the needs of others as well, using Scripture.

Over the years, we've had the privilege of hosting missionaries, pastors and their families, and other servants of the Lord in our home, including my husband's students, staff members in the churches we attended, as well as Christian friends who were going on short or long-term mission assignments seeking support and encouragement. This has been a wonderful opportunity for our children to see how people have dedicated their lives to serve Him. They've seen up close that missionaries are people with needs and questions, just like the rest of us, and have been able to interact with them about the Lord's work. They've also seen us come alongside those servants of God with encouragement and occasionally even financial support.

Serving Together

One thing we've found to be particularly important for spiritual nurture and growth is serving together as a family. As I get occasional invitations to speak at local churches, I welcome one or several of my children to accompany me. In this way, the children feel they are a vital part of the ministry and see firsthand what serving the Lord looks like.

Rather than feeling like ministry pulls us away from them, let's include our children in some of the ways in which we serve the Lord. Let's not merely encourage our children to read the Bible and pray. We also want to encourage them to serve as an outflow of loving God in the local church and in mission and ministry, and ideally, we can do at least some of this together as a family.

Discipling and Mentoring Our Children

Discipling and mentoring our children is a complex task. We believe that the Great Commission given by Jesus to make disciples starts at home. If we're not resolved to disciple our own children, crossing an ocean to go on a mission trip or ministering to others at the price of neglecting our own family is a travesty. That said, we can disciple and mentor our children only to the extent that they're receptive. In so doing, we've found that there is a certain gender-specific dimension that is crucial to observe. There are ways in which our daughters find it easier to confide in their mother, especially on topics more directly related to women: female issues, medical questions, modest clothing, inner beauty, and relationships, etc. The same kind of dynamic is at work with our sons and their father. We recognize, too, that the girls often desire the input and the shoulder of their father, and the boys love their mom and respect her wisdom on life matters. This is just part of the complexity of children growing and various needs arising and changing over time.

When the boys reached a certain age—between twelve and fourteen—they tended to gravitate increasingly toward their dad and crave male companionship and mentoring. No disrespect toward their mother, but they needed man-to-man sharpening. This was not merely a matter of socializing or watching sporting events together, or of other recreational pursuits such as fishing or camping, but also involved dealing with matters emerging in adolescence such as temptation, confidence issues related to their performance in team or individual sports, and general decision-making, scheduling, and career decisions, which becomes increasingly important in the upper high school and early college years.

Asking Questions

Of the two of us, Margaret is the more detail oriented; I'm a bit more of a big picture person. Whenever our children come home from some event, she excels at asking specific and caring questions about what happened:

'Where was it?'

'How many people were there?'

'Who did you sit next to?'

'What happened?'

'What did you talk about?'

'Were there any problems or challenges?'

My wife's penchant for asking detailed questions never ceases to amaze me. In this way, she can stay in close touch with our children and draw them out. At first, give them time as they may be reluctant to talk, but after a while they'll be fully engaged and typically start sharing freely.

Teachable Moments

When mentoring our children, we particularly enjoy using teachable moments. Not that there are always easy answers, and just being there is a huge part of the ministry to our children, but in short there are often clear directions we can give to them.

Did the referee make a bad call in your child's game? Life isn't always fair. We can argue the call (which will most likely be unsuccessful) or choose to move on and keep playing the game and let your character and skills do the talking.

Did someone else get the position your child applied for? In the end, God is sovereign, and He'll do what He knows is best for us.

Did a friend disappoint them or turn against them? We know it hurts, but people will often disappoint you, so put your trust in God—the only One who'll never let you down.

Did you get a traffic ticket? Accept responsibility for your actions and pay up.

Did you have a difficult day? With God, there are ultimately no bad days because He can use all things to accomplish his purposes, even if it feels bad.

Got a bad grade? Did you do your best? If so, keep at it. If not, you may need to be more diligent. And always, let's keep things in perspective.

Something broke? We can buy another plate or glass. Nobody died. Be careful not to exaggerate the problem.

You've got a problem, even a serious problem? We've got a lot to be grateful for. Be thankful your family has good health and in poor health trust God and do the next thing.

Were you involved in an accident? No one got seriously hurt. If so, we're together in this and God is with us and for us—our ultimate hope and strength.

Over the course of a child's growing up years, there are literally thousands of teachable moments, dozens every day, which wise, thoughtful, and committed parents can use to reinforce a biblical perspective and worldview. You don't have to generate teachable moments—only recognize and seize upon those that life brings your way.

Practical Ideas

Intentionally equipping your son or daughter to grow spiritually may involve the study of a book or specific topic in the Bible with them. You may choose to go out or meet with them individually once or twice a week to discuss spiritual and personal matters. Though much of what took place in our family in terms of making disciples of our children occurred in the natural context of living in relationship, there were times when setting formal goals was helpful.

If you have the opportunity to facilitate a study (or have a qualified parent help you) in apologetics (defending the faith) or hermeneutics (how to study the Bible) for sons or daughters in small groups, this can be extremely valuable. With careful planning, and facilitated conscientiously, these series of meetings might be considered for homeschool credit. In any case, these are golden opportunities to intentionally equip your child strategically for a lifetime of studying God's Word and sharing their faith.

When the children were in their preteen and teenage years, Andreas also led a family Bible study following the Sunday service. Intentionally involving parents along with their children both in terms of fellowship and teaching allowed the younger generation to learn from the insights of the more mature generation, but there was always mutual sharing as well. There was breakfast, prayer, and instruction together every Sunday, as well as occasional times dedicated to evening prayer on Sunday. We greatly valued this period of our lives where time of worship and learning occurred together.

Conclusion

Introduce your child to Christ. Pray actively for your child's salvation and look for opportunities to explain the gospel to him or her. Realize that if your child is not a believer, you'll need to rely on external moral instruction, discipline, in all love and kindness, as well as other ways of influencing your child, which is both fair and necessary. The expectations are still there because of God's holy and just character. If anything, this might drive a child to their knees to seek God's help, just like the law aimed to lead the people of Israel to Christ.

Once your child has trusted Christ and received the Holy Spirit, then the Spirit will do His work to convict, guide, and teach your child internally, transforming their thinking and desires in a Godward direction. Not that this will solve all your problems as a parent, of course, but the Spirit will prove not only to be a powerful ally in the parenting task, but the power in which you and your children live out their lives for the Lord.

We know that is sometimes easier said than done, and in the end God's purposes are sovereign and inscrutable. God won't always conform to our expectations, and we also must leave the timing to Him. We may do everything right and still reap an ungrateful and rebellious child in return. Esau may or may not have had amazing parenting but before he was born, already in the womb, it was known what kind of person he would be. At other times, we may make mistakes and yet God may be amazingly gracious and cover for our shortcomings.

Parenting can't be reduced to a formula—If you do A, B will happen. Human relationships are complex, especially in a world controlled by the 'ruler of this world,' which puts sinful people together in sinful families and communities in this imperfect world. And yet, if our child has a personal relationship with Christ, his eternal destiny is secure: 'The Lord is my light and my salvation; whom shall I fear? The Lord is the stronghold of my life; of whom shall I be afraid?' (Ps. 27:1). If they're genuinely converted, and regenerated, they're God's own possession, and we can trust Him to guide and take care of them, with us parents as His instruments and guides along the way.

♦ *How would you assess the current spiritual condition of your children? Do you believe they have trusted Christ? If not, what do you think is the reason why they have yet to trust Christ? If so, do your children live out their faith or have they yet to grasp the implications of their commitment?*

♦ *What can you do to introduce your children to Christ or, if they are believers already, how can you encourage them in their relationship with Christ? Is there a book you would like to go through with them on a specific topic?*

♦ *Identify at least three teachable moments you encountered with your children during the last week or two. How did you seize these moments to help them become more Christlike in the way they handled adversity or in some other way?*

5

Child and Parent

Presence is an essential quality in parenting. Parents have the privilege of cultivating a growing, trusting relationship with their children, exercising 'holy love.' The parenting relationship is lifelong, and though it changes over time it never ends. Read the following passages and reflect on how your presence in your child's life matters.

♦ *Read Deuteronomy 6:4-9. What does this passage tell us about God's conception of parenting?*

♦ *Read John 15:12-15. Applied to parenting, what should be our primary focus in relating to our children per this passage?*

Parenting is more than a defined task to be accomplished whereby parenting goals are clearly identified, achieved, and measured. It is also larger than applying the most effective method of discipline to produce a well-behaved child. Rather, parenting is in large part a growing, intimate, and trusting relationship with your child of supporting and equipping them for life. Since every child is unique, parents of multiple children need to be sensitive to encourage, and even discipline in different ways. One-size parenting rarely fits all! Since children (especially at a younger age) typically crave their parents' presence and it is evident that *many* lessons are caught rather than taught, we aim to spend much time with our children and be their friend (not in a child-centered but a God-centered kind of way). Practicing a relational approach to parenting results in personal and spiritual rewards that are palpable, pleasing, and powerful.

A Father's Presence

Recent reports highlight the scourge of fatherlessness in the United States and the UK and point out the serious implications for children's education and many other areas of life. There are not only tremendous social and economic costs but relational and spiritual ones as well.

According to the U.S. Census Bureau, an astounding 24.7 million children don't live with their biological father. The Department of Education states that 39 per cent of students in grades 1 through 12 are fatherless. In an interview, David Blankstein, a veteran educator, states that children without a father are four times as likely to be poor and twice as likely to drop out of school. A recent study entitled 'The Vital Importance of Paternal Presence in Children's Lives' indicates that seven out of ten high school dropouts lack the presence of their father. Girls without a father are twice as likely to be obese and four times as likely to get pregnant in their teens. In terms of racial demographics, fatherlessness is at 20 per cent for Caucasians, 31 per cent for Hispanics, and 57 per cent for African-Americans.

The situation in the UK is not much different. According to the Relationships Foundation 'Cost of Family Failure Index,' family breakdown in 2016 cost £48 billion or £1,820 per taxpayer, exceeding the entire defense budget. The Centre for Social Justice reports in a study entitled 'Fractured Families: Why Stability Matters,' that half of all children born in the UK are raised by only one parent, typically the mother. Not only do a million British children grow up with 'no meaningful contact at all' with their fathers, there is a 'dearth' of male teachers in British schools. As a result, many children from fatherless homes struggle in school or drop out altogether, battle low self-esteem, have a tough time making friends, and are afflicted with anxiety or depression.

This data provides compelling statistical support for what is intuitively obvious and biblically indicated: A father's presence is vital for a child's flourishing, not only socially but spiritually as well, especially during the growing up years and adolescence. We've already observed at the beginning of our book that the very notion of parenthood is grounded in God and who He is as our creator and heavenly Father. At this point in our discussion, let's further explore the notion of the fatherhood of God in terms of how God the Father and His presence with His people serves as a paradigm for the way in which *parents'* presence in children's lives is a key aspect of parenting.

The Bible is full of references to God's presence. Living in God's presence is depicted as tantamount to being blessed, while being expelled from God's presence—as happened to Adam and Eve at the Fall (and will happen to unbelievers at the end of time)—is being utterly undone. As church father Augustine of Hippo famously remarked, 'You have made us for yourself, O Lord, and our souls are restless until they find their rest in you.' As a matter of fact, the Bible's entire story revolves around God's presence. The story is essentially about human beings created for the purpose of living in God's presence, then being expelled from God's presence, and in Christ being reconciled to God and finally, through the Spirit, being enabled to live in God's presence once again.

Parenting, too, is primarily about presence—the parents' presence with their children (and, of course, God's presence with *us* as we parent). In some ways that should be intuitive, and probably won't take too much convincing. If you're a parent, you'll *want* to spend a lot of time with your children because you genuinely enjoy being with them, for the most part. The problem is, you're busy, you've got to make a living, you have other passions you want to pursue, and you still have a marriage to cultivate while being a parent. So, for many of us, it's not so much a matter of desire as it's a matter of feasibility and the pressures of life crowding in that make the reality of parenting different from the ideal.

That's why we have confidence that 'parenting as presence' will make a substantial difference in your life experience as a parent. You see, it's easier to keep parenting at arm's length when the baby is small, especially for the dad (though there are also many dads who help a lot). You can have your cake—keep working hard at your job, go out on dates, play some golf—while your wife does most of the 'heavy lifting' such as nursing the baby, changing the diapers, and making sure the little one is properly cared for in every way. And you can eat it, too—enjoy the romance of having a child with the one you love, take some endearing family pictures, and uphold the gratifying vision that yours is a happy, healthy family.

It's easy for some fathers to excuse themselves from being present in the family by spending an inordinate amount of time on providing for the family. This mistake can be made even by strong believers who prioritize providing for their families, but because of a demanding career and church commitments, the children end up not seeing much of dad. And he may be exhausted when they do finally get to spend time together. In a father's mind, he may think he is present *by* providing, and to some degree that is true, but the family may experience his absence profoundly, and see him providing *instead of* being present. While it is essential for fathers to provide for their families, fathers need to take care to balance work with their children's need to be in his presence.

A Mother's Presence

In a culture saturated with feminism and egalitarianism, the value of a mother staying home with her children is typically undervalued. The resulting neglect is especially poignant during the child's most formative years. This gaping hole has significant ramifications not only for the child's life, but also the mother's. A child left to the care of another person may possibly end up developing in a rather different direction and the mother will lack the intended fulfillment and blessing meant for her as well as the significant impact on the world she might otherwise have.

We encourage you to *embrace the role God gave you. Don't be distracted by what the world says will bring you more satisfaction.* Despite any efforts to rationalize the decision as a new mother to go right back to work, or to employ the services of nannies or day-care centers, even church-based ones, there's just no adequate justification for placing expediency, lifestyle, self-promotion, or other considerations above God's primary calling and His purpose for you as a mother.

The Bible specifies the God-given design for the woman in the creation narrative, including her distinct and indispensable purpose (Genesis 1–2, esp. 2:18, 20). This role as wife and mother resounds throughout the entire creation account, even in that of the Fall, where God's judgment on her consists in sanctions that reinforce her God-given roles—pain in *childbirth* and *relational* struggle in her *marriage* (i.e., a desire to control; Gen. 3:16).

The very name 'Eve' in Hebrew means '*mother* of all the living' (Gen. 3:20). The command given at the very beginning to be 'fruitful and multiply' (Gen. 1:28) indicates that *procreation* is at the heart of God's purpose for man and woman in marriage. The *nurturing role* implied as a role for the woman, as well as the creating of a *home* environment where her family can thrive. Observe also the signposts of a woman's stature that point to her God-given function of nurturing children in her feminine reproductive build. If we respect the woman's biological function of giving birth to children and her capacity to nurse and care for an infant, we will make room for her to be there for her child in the way God created her. Let her be a woman!

Jesus said, 'No one can serve two masters,' adding, 'You cannot serve God and money' (Matt. 6:24; Luke 16:13). Similarly, we'd argue that as a woman you can't be all God intended a mother to be and put your career first at the same time. Choices must be made, and these may involve some personal sacrifices. Unfortunately, many don't realize that parenting requires this kind of sacrifice (or they are in denial in this regard), thinking they can enjoy the benefits of being a parent without counting the cost. Jesus also said that anyone who would build a tower better first count the cost (Luke 14:28); the same is true for parenting. And yet, whatever sacrifice parents are called to make for their children is far outweighed in the long run by the joy and rewards yielded by the investment in their children.

So, let's not be shortsighted and put short-term interests above a long-term perspective on parenting. No childcare substitute can ever adequately replace the mother's presence with her children during their growing years. Those who abide by and joyfully embrace God's plan will be blessed, as will the children. Such families may stand out in a culture that often fails to acknowledge the wisdom, goodness, and beauty of God's design, and in so doing, will testify to the God who designed the family, and will participate in His mission, glorifying God, and ultimately pointing them to their Creator.

Parents vs. Peers

Despite the vital importance of a father's and mother's presence with their children, we've observed that children, far too early in their young lives, are removed from their parents' care and influence in various ways. Gradually, peers rival parents' influence, and eventually parents are relegated to the sidelines. In many cases, this happens all too soon and earlier than it should. Parents may still be cheerleaders, but the children are calling all the plays on the field. Yet not all the plays work, and often they would benefit from our experienced input and guidance.

It's certainly healthy for them to make their own decisions before God, and we should give them space to do so, though daughters, particularly, will benefit if they remain under the father's guidance and protection until they marry. Adult children should appreciate the wisdom God has given parents—particularly, but not exclusively, if they're walking with God. As the book of Proverbs tells us repeatedly, the wise person will seek guidance; in the multitude of counselors there is wisdom (Prov. 11:14; 15:22; 24:6).

Have you been able to instill discretion on key matters and genuine wisdom in your child? Wisdom in young people is an increasingly rare commodity. At its core, Proverbs is written to impart wisdom to the 'simple' young person who needs instruction—especially young men—so they can get on a godly path for life and find a godly wife. In many ways, the purpose of parenting is integrally bound up with equipping your children to make good decisions so they can find and live out their mission and God-given purpose for their lives.

When They're Adolescents

In his book, *Age of Opportunity*, Paul Tripp talks about the importance of hanging out with our children while they're getting to be comfortable with their identity during the teenage years. He talks about parents staying up late into the night and spending hours talking to their teenage son or daughter—that's the love language they crave. It doesn't come as naturally for me as it does for my wife, but I've come to see that this is one important way we show our children that we care. We spend time with them and come alongside them and help them figure things out. Or, at least we're friends, confidantes, and sounding boards for their thinking and struggles.

Fathers, it may be a good idea to anticipate extra demands on your time during the all-important teenage years in your children's lives and arrange your schedule accordingly. Try to make every effort to attend special occasions such as recitals, games, graduations, or moving them into their dorm room in college. It could also mean deciding to school your children at home, which will give you many extra hours with them.

The book of Proverbs tells us that young people characteristically are simple, naïve, or foolish and desperately need continual instruction and guidance (Prov. 1:4). Those who are responsive to wise instruction will gradually *grow* wise—especially if they surround themselves with wise and like-minded others—while those who are resistant will become increasingly foolish and suffer the consequences of their unwise choices (Prov. 13:20).

If you adopt a relational approach to parenting, you may find that, whether they say it or not, your college-age children often need extra support and encouragement during this exciting and challenging time. Your support can take various forms—wisdom and guidance in choosing a course of study or classes, studying with them for exams, going shopping with them, offering advice concerning relationships or career choices, among other things.

Being There for Them

Again, the fatherhood of God will be our foundational model in terms of providing, protecting, and shepherding as well as nurturing and caring for them. Just as God reassures His people, 'I will be with you,' so we can be there for our children. When Joshua was about to enter, and conquer, the promised land, God promised to be with him

(Josh. 1:8-9). In the book of Hebrews, we read: 'Be content with what you have, for he has said, "I will never leave you nor forsake you." So we can confidently say, "The Lord is my helper; I will not fear; what can man do to me?"' (Heb. 13:6-7). Have more encouraging words ever been spoken? In the same way, we can assure our children that we'll always be with them, to the extent God gives us the opportunity. We can't always *literally* be with them, nor would they want us to. But we can be available and we can pray.

Parenting as presence doesn't necessarily mean that we'll always be by their side at every moment. The relationship obviously changes over time. As they mature, it may mean simply being there for them when they need us. We want our children to know that we'll always be there for them, no matter what, to the best of our ability, and according to God's provision. We're prepared to comfort them when they need comfort. We love to celebrate their successes with them and to help them learn from their failures. As grandparents, we'll gladly watch their children for them, giving them time for refreshment (I remember so desperately desiring this support as a young mom).

Also, one day we'll die. But we can *remain* with them even in the values and principles we have instilled in them, and through the character and wisdom we imparted: 'Train up a child in the way he should go; even when he is old he will not depart from it' (Prov. 22:6). In this way, we can be our children's best friend: 'A friend loves at all times, and a brother is born for adversity' (Prov. 17:17). This is true even when we must confront our children and speak the truth to them in love: 'Faithful are the wounds of a friend' (Prov. 27:6).

The Mentoring Mandate

The essence of what we're trying to convey here can be illustrated by biblical and spiritual example, specifically that of Paul the apostle. Like a parent, Paul was always there for his spiritual children and mentees, cultivating a growing, trusting relationship with them. He mentored young men such as Timothy and Titus (2 Tim. 3:10-11; Titus 2; 3:1-12) and sent them out as his apostolic delegates. While they were serving in a different location, Paul was committed to staying in touch. Whenever he could, he visited them to see how things were going. When this was impossible, he would send a caring letter, with expressions of personal affection, words of encouragement, and helpful instructions. In this way, in keeping with ancient custom, Paul's letters became a substitute for his presence.

Over the years, Paul continued to be present in the lives and ministry of his spiritual children and those whom he had mentored in the faith. In addition, he regularly prayed for these individuals (2 Tim. 1:3). The same principle applies to our natural children, especially those who, by God's grace, have been converted and now also are our brothers and sisters in Christ.

Thus, in truth, if you have children, parenting is a lifelong calling. We can never check off 'parenting' on our To-Do list. Mentoring never really ends. It continues way past our children's middle school and high school years into their adult lives, and in many cases even into the lives of our grandchildren. Even when we die, the impact we have had on our children during our lifetime continues in their lives and through them in the lives of their children, both natural and spiritual, and so forth. This is the beauty of God's plan for us as we reproduce in kind, after His image, and in His likeness, for His glory. How profoundly wise and attractive God's design is for us as parents who seek to live our lives in keeping with His creation purpose.

Conclusion

Presence is the essence of parenting. If you think you can parent in maintenance mode, you're on borrowed time, and your lack of commitment to truly 'showing up' as a parent will catch up with you sooner or later. It may take some time before you pay a price, but eventually you will.

Be there for your child. Cultivate a growing, trusting relationship with him. Love him—biblically defined—and be his friend. There'll inevitably be rough and challenging times, but if you're fully engaged—which takes time, lots of it—you'll be able to help him make it through and teach him abiding lessons along the way. This, in turn, will build character and equip your child to grow in his ability to make wise, well-informed, and balanced decisions. Be a relational parent: Can there be any other kind?

For us, we mentored our children as they were growing up, trying to instill in them our values and biblical principles, especially regarding living the Christian life and making wise decisions. We've found that even now that most of our children have moved or gone to college, there is a sense in which we can still be present with them. Wherever they will be in the future, we will continue to be 'present' with them through these abiding principles and values.

We can also be present with them through diverse types of contact long distance, whether skype, texting, phone calls, or other means. In this way, we can continue our relationship with them, providing further mentoring and equipping.

Also, we're present with them through occasional visits. They may visit us, or we may visit them. These can be close times of reconnecting and of heart-to-heart sharing that are mutually beneficial and encouraging but continue the parent-child relationship, albeit now among grown individuals.

Finally, we remain 'present' with them as we uphold them in prayer.

♦ *Reflect on whether you have sufficient time to spend with your children. If not, what can you do to make time for them? What keeps you from being the dad or mom God wants you to be?*

♦ *Discuss: Do you conceive of parenting as a relationship or as a task/job to be accomplished, or a combination of the two? Do you need to make any adjustments in the way you view your role as a parent and, if so, what course of action should you pursue?*

♦ *What are some things you could do with your children? Spend some time brainstorming possible activities and make a list. Then, plan to follow through on your ideas. Consult your children as well; they will be glad to help you.*

6
Child and Others

In parenting, conflict is inevitable, both between spouses and between parents and children. With God's help, families can resolve conflict with help from following a simple 4-step process of conflict resolution. As you read the following passages, reflect on the true source of all our conflict and how families can deal with conflict by putting on the spiritual armor of God.

> ♦ *Read James 4:1-6. What is the cause of conflict in your family? How is real progress in handling conflict possible?*
>
> ♦ *Read Ephesians 6:10-18. How does this passage on spiritual warfare apply to family life? In what ways does Satan attempt to wreak havoc and what should be our strategy?*

Disagreements over parenting and financial issues are the most common causes of marital conflict. If parenting and conflict are close twins, let's make every effort to address this need. This is even more called for in view of the value that our Lord placed on peacemaking when he said, 'Blessed are the peacemakers, for they shall be called sons of God' (Matt. 5:9).

When we started having children, we hammered out a joint parenting philosophy over many hours of (at times passionate) discussion over every subject from ways of disciplining children, to choosing edifying movies, and a plethora of other issues. At the time, this seemed tedious, if not a distraction or even a waste of time. Looking back, however, we realize that God led us through a process of exchanging thoughts, dreams, and struggles with each other; so much so that we've grown closer together as a couple and have gradually become more and more united in our approach to guiding our children—God's precious gifts to us.

In this book, you've seen us advocate a realistic and relational approach. Both aspects of parenting—realism and relationship—entail the recognition that conflict is a constant reality, even in the life of committed Christian parents of children who are believers (and certainly unbelievers). Effective conflict resolution is vital, and a conflict avoidance strategy is doomed to fail. This requires peacemaking skills and a strong trust in the sovereignty and power of God.

God makes no mistakes; He knows the end from the beginning, and He is a forgiving and loving God. We need to learn to look at things from *His* perspective and seek to discern *His* purpose in our circumstances. We also need to learn to deal with our sinful nature, be aware of spiritual realities and then engage in spiritual warfare. In all of this, we need to pray.

The Reality of Conflict

One of the most impressive features of the Bible is again its realism. There just isn't simply a rosy, artificial picture of what life on earth is like, but rather it tells it like it is. From the very beginning of human existence, we know that Satan introduced conflict and strife into our relationships with God and one another. When God first held the man, and then the woman, accountable for transgressing His command not to eat the forbidden fruit in the Garden, both failed to accept responsibility for their sin. Instead, they blamed somebody else.

Take a quick look. God said to the man: '"Have you eaten of the tree of which I commanded you not to eat?" The man said, "The woman whom you gave to be with me, she gave me fruit of the tree, and I ate." Then the LORD God said to the woman, "What is this that you have done?" The woman said, "The serpent deceived me, and I ate"' (Gen. 3:11-13).

Incredibly, in his response to God, the man manages to blame not only the *woman* for his sin but even *God Himself*: 'the woman whom *you* gave me.' Then, when the *woman* is held to account, she blames the *serpent* (i.e., Satan). This failure to accept responsibility for our actions has been part of human experience on this earth ever since.

Similarly, very early in human history, sibling rivalry was first recorded when Cain killed Abel, his brother (Genesis 4).

Later, during the exodus, Moses confronted his brother Aaron for making an idol for the people of Israel in form of a golden calf. Again, rather than accepting responsibility, Aaron said this: 'So I said to them, "Let any who have gold take it off." So they gave it to me, and I threw it into the fire, and out came this calf' (Exod. 32:22-24). What a lame excuse!

I'm sure some of you who are parents have heard similar tall tales when confronting your children about something they did wrong. While it's hard to keep a straight face when these kinds of ridiculous excuses are dished out, they illustrate the problem with our sinful human nature: We have a tough time accepting responsibility for our own actions, and when confronted, we tend to put the blame on others.

Don't Be Surprised

Realistic parenting will expect conflict. We shouldn't be surprised when disagreements arise. Relational parenting requires that we pay proper attention to conflict and deal with it rather than sweeping it under the rug. In the family in which you grew up, what was the normal mechanism for conflict resolution? In some families, conflict is simply ignored. Many seem to be afraid of any form of discord. Others erupt in anger, or even violence, only to later apologize and vow never to resort to anger or violence again. Sadly, while their intentions may be commendable, keeping this kind of unrealistic promise is virtually impossible. What should we do when conflict occurs?

Steps of Conflict Resolution

You may want to consider the following four principles of conflict resolution we attempt to practice in our home.

1. Analyze the issue: Identifying the problem in the relationship is a vital step toward conflict resolution. This may take some time because the parties may not see eye to eye on what happened and where the responsibility for the conflict lies. Ask questions, then listen. As parents, we should try to mediate and ensure fairness while not taking sides in the conflict. Focusing on blame rather than restoration also can add insult to injury causing unnecessary and extended conflict. If your children genuinely perceive you as an honest broker who desires their best, rather than being negative, partial, or overbearing in the adjudication of wrongs, this will go a long way toward bringing the two parties together. Take the necessary time to cover the details but don't overanalyze. Dwelling on the problem can cause exasperation and desperation in the person sinning and unnecessarily draw the family into further conflict. Be judicious and wise here, loving and kind remembering that kindness leads to repentance (Rom. 2:4). As you take time to assess what happened, it may be helpful to take some time-out (even if just a few minutes), especially if you've pushed too hard in getting your children to do something you wanted them to do or if you've been pushed beyond your limits by them.

2. Accept responsibility for your actions: Once we've identified what happened and what the issue is, the next step is for each of the persons involved to accept responsibility for their own actions. In some, if not most cases, there may be just one person responsible for the conflict, or at least one main perpetrator of the incident; however, there is often wrongdoing to be admitted on the part of more than one party in the conflict. God made us responsible agents; whether we admit it or not, we are *each* responsible for our actions. Guiding each of our children to accept responsibility for what they've done may be hard but, with appropriate balance and attention to the emotional dynamics of the situation, will go a long way toward effective conflict resolution.

3. Apologize as needed: Now that you've identified the issue and people have accepted responsibility for what they have done, it's time to apologize. Apologies should be offered voluntarily and freely. Allow your children time to come to terms with what they've done and accept responsibility for their actions. If they genuinely need help, guide them in formulating a meaningful, heartfelt apology. Giving them thirty seconds to apologize won't always work. They are living, breathing, thinking, and feeling human beings who need to go through a natural process of repentance and asking for forgiveness, which takes time. Over time, families able to practice reconciliation on a regular basis will develop skills for restoring relationships effectively, save a lot of unproductive time in arguing, and prevent unnecessary tearing down of self-worth and confidence of family members. Parents who apologize first set the tone for the family. Your role model is so important in family dynamics. Apologize! Apologize! Apologize!

4. Affirm your love and affection: The last step in effective conflict resolution is reaffirming love for one another and reconciling the relationship. Give each other a hug if it comes naturally, tell each other how much you appreciate each other, and explain how the offense, however hurtful, was not intended to convey any disrespect or lack of affection. It has often been our experience that after conflict has been resolved, the relationship can be even deeper and more meaningful than it was before. In fact, there is genuine personal and relational *healing* that results when conflict is truly and effectively resolved: 'Therefore, confess your sins to one another and pray for one another, that you may be *healed*' (James 5:16). Just like a fractured bone, when healed, becomes stronger than before the fracture, so a healed relationship can be stronger if the issue is truly resolved.

Principles of Conflict Resolution

Step	Action	Explanation
1	Analyze the issue	Ask questions. Listen. Identify the problem to find out what happened and who is responsible
2	Accept responsibility for your actions	Everyone should accept responsibility for what they did rather than blaming others
3	Apologize as needed	Issue a meaningful, heartfelt apology for what you did to hurt another person
4	Affirm your love and affection	Reaffirm one's love and reconcile relationship with the other person

Managing Anger

A particularly thorny issue to deal with when it comes to conflict is anger. The Bible tells us not to sin when we're angry (Eph. 4:26). In fact, there's such a thing as righteous anger or indignation in the face of glaring injustice. Certainly, Jesus exhibited such righteous anger when cleansing the temple, not once but twice, when witnessing the defilement of the worship of God through commercialism and profiteering (Mark 11:15-17; John 2:13-22). But none of us is the sinless Son of God, so even when we do witness genuine injustice, we may not always be pure in the way we respond. This is what Jesus was talking about when He called on people to take the log out of their own eye before trying to take the speck out of the eye of another person (Matt. 7:5; Luke 6:42).

Apart from the obvious humor, Jesus's comment reflects incredible insight into the human dilemma. Often, when we see a problem in another person's life, the reason why we're attuned to that problem is because we ourselves have that problem! If I'm irked by someone's competitiveness, or arrogance, I should ask myself: Why does this other person's flaw irritate and annoy me so much? Could it be that I have the same problem? More likely than not, I do. Even if I don't, I should be careful in the way I confront the other person. God's Word tells us to restore others in a spirit of gentleness (Gal. 6:1-2; 2 Tim. 2:25). It also tells those who think they stand to be careful so they don't fall (1 Cor. 10:12).

All of this is to say that most of the time, our anger may not be undiluted, justified anger, but at best be a combination of both righteous indignation and envy or pride or some other sinful motivation. In parenting, it'll be vital to help our children work through their anger in a way that gets to the heart of the problem. What's the cause of their anger: Is it motivated by selfishness or have they been wronged in some way? Are they angry because they didn't get their way or is there some wrong that was perpetrated that we must address? If the former, this will give us as parents an opportunity to help them come to terms with their selfishness and urge them on to a Christlike spirit (assuming they're Christians; if not, we can pray that God may expose their selfishness to show them their need for the savior). If the latter, we should do everything we can to make things right.

That said, there'll be times when we're unable to undo harm that was done or bring people who have wronged our children to justice. In such instances, we'll need to teach our children to commit a situation, and other people, to the Lord, knowing that He is the judge and will ultimately call these people to account. The Bible teaches that we shouldn't retaliate but forgive those who have wronged us, following Christ's example who forgave those who put Him on the cross (Rom. 12:17-21; 1 Pet. 2:23-25). Dealing with the situation privately rather than publicly and acting swiftly will lessen the tension sooner rather than later (Matt. 18:15). Often problems grow worse if they're not dealt with promptly because the delay may allow Satan to gain a foothold in the relationship. He will exploit unresolved anger or bitterness and sow seeds of doubt and distrust, resulting in broken relationships that hinder God's blessing in our lives (Eph. 4:26-27, 31; cf. Heb. 12:15).

Practicing Forgiveness

The beautiful thing about having been introduced to a relationship with God in Christ, and having one's sins forgiven upon repentance and faith, is that we know we're all sinners and need forgiveness. This means that we've been forgiven and are in turn called to forgive others. In genuinely resolving conflict, there's nothing like the power of actual forgiveness. Importantly, the power of forgiveness comes from the blood of Christ which was shed when He died for us and in our place on the Cross. Teach your children to treasure the power of forgiveness. They've been forgiven, and they, in turn, can forgive others. What's more, whatever wrong is committed against them pales in comparison to what Jesus had to endure—He who lived a sinless life and was viciously vilified and crucified by sinners.

That said, the fact that Christians know the power of forgiveness doesn't mean that conflict resolution will be easy. Because we're human, and God has made us different—male and female, various personalities, backgrounds, etc.—there'll be plenty of room for misunderstanding, hurt feelings, and friction. The other day my daughter's feelings got hurt because my son didn't tell her some piece of personal information before telling some of his friends. It took them about half an hour over lunch—with some input from us—to sort out their differences. As it turned out, my son's neglect to tell his sister first was entirely unintentional, but her feelings were still hurt. What a valuable lesson for him for when he's married! Be thorough in working through those kinds of issues and take whatever time you need to get to the bottom of an issue to resolve it fairly.

Sources of Conflict

What are some of the major sources of conflict in families? It's been our experience that there's nothing too trivial to become a source of conflict. When you live in close quarters with one another day after day, it's easy for minor irritants to turn into major grudges. In addition, sources of conflict may include the following:

- **Dealing with social media:** what age to start, what to post or not to post, family privacy

- **Relationships:** issues related to dating, boyfriends or girlfriends, being left out of a social circle

- **Sibling rivalry:** alleged favoritism, parental inconsistency, territorial issues (invading or violating another person's space, not respecting their property)

- **Disobedience:** various kinds of insubordination, challenges of parental or other authority, rebelliousness

- **Insensitivity:** boys not treating girls in a respectful manner, being inconsiderate of another's feelings when they're tired or having a rough day, girls not affirming boys and encouraging them to lead

- **Miscommunication or no communication:** unwarranted assumptions, lack of clarity, unloving words

Knowing conflict is inevitable and taking steps to ensure the proper handling of it will go a long way toward creating the kind of goodwill that is vital to resolving conflict on a day-to-day basis.

Spiritual Warfare

Thus far, we've been talking about conflict primarily on a horizontal plane as occurring between two or more individuals. Of course, that's the way we perceive all conflict, and so we typically deal with it on a human level. As Christians, however, we also know that at times the source of conflict may be supernatural. The Bible attests to the fact that God didn't merely create humans but also supernatural spiritual beings called 'angels.' Some of the angels, the Bible tells us, subsequently rebelled against their Creator, including the highest angel, Lucifer or Satan, and his horde of demons. It's therefore possible that the opposition we're facing doesn't come from a mere human source but has a supernatural, evil, and demonic origin.

This calls for much wisdom and prayer. We've found that especially prior to major ministry engagements, spiritual opposition tends to grow more obvious and intense. The devil may try to exploit our vulnerability and weakness, or sheer busyness, by attacking us when we least expect it or are most susceptible to it. Often temptations come and are harder to deal with when we're tired after a long and exhausting day or vulnerable in some other way. At times, it may be a major victory or success that causes us to be overenthusiastic, unguarded, or careless, and before we know it, we've stumbled. Wise individuals will take the necessary precautions against supernatural attacks, including prayer, time in God's Word, accountability to others, and awareness of certain areas of weakness.

The most detailed passage on spiritual warfare in the Bible is found in Ephesians 6:10-18. Strikingly, the passage follows almost immediately the sections on the husband-wife and child-parent relationships in the letter. This underscores the vital connection between spiritual warfare on the one hand and marriage and family on the other. It's in these key areas that the spiritual battle between God and Satan rages most fiercely. At the core, the battle is for our minds: 'I am afraid that just as Eve was deceived by the serpent's cunning, your *mind*s may somehow be led astray from your sincere and pure devotion to Christ' (2 Cor. 11:3 NIV). The challenge, therefore, is this: to 'take captive every *thought* to make it obedient to Christ' (2 Cor. 10:3-5 NIV).

We need to teach our children that whenever they realize that they've begun to think a thought that is unspiritual, they can cut it off and refuse to continue thinking along those lines. Instead, they can pray and ask God to help them think thoughts that are pleasing to Him and in keeping with His will and values. In this way, they won't 'be conformed to this world, but be transformed by the renewal' of their mind (Rom. 12:2). Significantly, the conflicts that arise in our families may often be because of Satan's attempt to destroy God's design in our homes and to create disharmony and disunity, just as he did with the first man and woman in the Garden.

In my book *God, Marriage, and Family*, I talk about three important principles for engaging in spiritual warfare: realizing that there is a spiritual battle going on; knowing the enemy (2 Cor. 10:4; Eph. 6:11; 1 Pet. 5:8-9); and using proper spiritual weapons. As to the use of proper weapons in spiritual warfare, we've found it helpful to think of the weapons listed in Ephesians 6 in conjunction with our marriage, family, and role as parents:

- **Truth:** All family members must 'put off falsehood and speak truthfully' to one another yet speak 'the truth in love' and thus 'in all things grow up into him who is the head, that is, Christ.' In their speech, they should make every effort not to 'let any unwholesome talk' come out of their mouth 'but only what is helpful' for building each other up 'according to their needs' (Eph. 4:25, 15, 29 niv).

- **Righteousness:** Righteousness designates our right standing with God in and through Christ and our dealings with God and one another with honesty and integrity (Rom. 5:1, 9; 2 Cor. 5:21; Ps. 15). For this reason, it is only in marriages and families where both spouses and their children live in the power of the Spirit that God's will can be truly and consistently lived out (Eph. 5:18; Rom. 8:9).

- **Peace:** As believers, we've been given the peace of Christ in the Holy Spirit (John 14:27; 16:33). We know that we've been eternally forgiven and that we're sons and daughters of God, that we are at peace with God, and we can be at peace with each other and act as peacemakers in the world around us (John 1:12; 1 John 3:1; Rom. 5:1; Matt. 5:9; 2 Cor. 5:17-18).

- **Faith:** All family members should follow the Lord Jesus Christ in discipleship and learn to trust him to meet their needs and overcome adversity. Their overriding concern should not be material needs but the extension of God's rule in the world (Matt. 6:25-34). Faith in God also entails trusting the Holy Spirit to perform his character-transforming work and to lead our children to a godly spouse.

- **Salvation:** Because believers in a family are assured of their salvation and eternal destiny, they can love each other unconditionally and selflessly. The husband can lead lovingly and responsibly, and the wife can trust and submit graciously to God's leading of her through her husband, so children see godly role models as they themselves hope to be married one day (Eph. 5:21-33).

- **The Word of God:** Because there is no lasting foundation for our lives apart from God's Word (Matt. 7:24-27; Heb. 4:12-13; 1 Pet. 1:23-25), a married couple and their children must be committed to 'remain in God's word' (John 8:31; 15:4, 7) through regular personal and joint Bible study and faithful attendance of and participation in a local church where the Word of God is preached (2 Tim. 4:2).

- **Prayer:** Regular joint prayer is essential in families to 'keep the unity of the Spirit through the bond of peace' (Eph. 4:3). Families should make a habit of bringing their thanksgiving and requests before God and trust Him to act on their behalf (Phil. 4:6-7; 1 Pet. 5:7). In exceptional circumstances, a couple or family may even choose to refrain from sexual relations for a time of concentrated prayer (1 Cor. 7:5).

Conclusion

As a realistic and relational parent, expect occasional or even frequent conflict and prepare to deal with it prayerfully, patiently, painstakingly, and lovingly. God has given us families and children to live life with. We need to welcome challenges as opportunities to grow and mature as individuals. Let's not shy away from conflict. If we fail to address and resolve issues as they arise, resentment may fester, and we'll be living with a ticking time bomb that'll explode when we least expect it and are least prepared to deal with it.

With your spouse, discuss questions such as these: How can we model effective conflict resolution? How will we deal with conflict among our children? What are the types of conflict that arise most frequently, and how can these be addressed successfully? Husband and wife must first learn to effectively model conflict resolution. Being able to deal with conflict effectively is one of the most important marks of realistic and relational parenting.

♦ *Is conflict a rare or common occurrence in your family? If the latter, what are some of the most common causes of conflict and what can you do to change that?*

♦ *Growing up, how did you typically deal with conflict in your family? Did your parents tend to try to avoid or ignore conflict or did they acknowledge it and try to resolve it? What were some of the major sources of conflict?*

♦ *What can you do to resolve conflict more effectively in your family, first between husband and wife, then parents to children and among two or more children?*

Part 3
RESPONSIBLE PARENTING

Guiding your Children toward Responsible Adulthood

The third tension we encounter as parents is that of assuming responsibility for our children's development rather than falling into a laissez-faire approach, essentially abandoning them to potentially harmful influences and their own devices and wisdom (or lack thereof). Now that we've learned how to parent realistically and relationally, we'll see the importance of guiding and developing our children in the way they should go morally, relationally, and vocationally. We must not abandon them to the winds of the culture and evil spiritual forces. Irresponsible parenting delegates a child's development to others: non-Christian teachers, even Christian schools, immature peers, youth pastors, celebrity role models, or Hollywood. Not that all of these are unimportant, but let's stand up and be counted. That goes both for absentee fathers who give their best hours to their company while wife and children get the leftovers and for mothers who don't embrace their God-given role of being with their children during their most formative years.

It's so easy to get sidetracked and caught up in the minutiae of everyday life as a parent. You make sure your children have all their checkups at the family doctor's office. You ensure they're not left behind socially, secure their place on a soccer or baseball team, and maybe have them learn an instrument (or two). There are countless practices and lessons to prepare for, not to mention birthday parties to attend. And for each of these parties you need to buy a present, or at least get a birthday card and/or gift card. Then, there are the various birthdays of your own children, as well as other holidays, to celebrate, including Thanksgiving (if you live in North America) and Christmas. Your social calendar is full. In fact, it's bursting at the seams!

Yet you can only kick the can down the road for so long. Eventually *ad hoc* parenting will catch up with you, and your children will carry on without you as their social coordinator. They may turn out to be driven, selfish, or even ruthless individuals who end up not even taking the time to take care of you or visit you in a nursing home at the end of your days! Does this sound too gloomy? We're aware of family situations where this has been the sad outcome. Therefore, it's critical not to succumb to the tyranny of the urgent and to put first things first; and that first thing, as we'll see, is character.

In addition, as parents you'll be called to guide your children's education. What's the relationship between character development and education? This is too important a question not to think through carefully as parents. Your child may get a good education—but is their character being developed, and if so, in what way? Finally, as parents, you can and should have a vital hand in equipping your child for life. You can help them discern their God-given calling and discover their mission in life. You can encourage them to assess and exercise their spiritual gifts so they can use them in the church. You can equip them for their marriage and vocation. Seeing the end from the beginning will hopefully give you the needed perspective and purpose.

7
Character

Character is who a person is at the very core of their being. It affects all their relationships and accomplishments in life. Character in our children doesn't just happen; parents must be intentional and make it a focus to guide character development in their children.

As you read the following passages, reflect on the immense value of character formation in the life of your child and the role both God and parents play in this regard.

♦ *Read Romans 5:1-5. What engenders godly character and what is the basis for our right standing before God? What difference does that make?*

♦ *Read Hebrews 12:4-13. What can we learn from this passage's teaching on God's loving exercise of discipline regarding developing character in our children?*

Many parents put a primary focus on their child's education. While education is important, such a focus on education is ultimately wrong-headed. Instead, after salvation and establishing children in their faith, parents' central concern should be on their child's character. Through children's various life stages (infant, toddler, preteen, teen, young adult), parents have the responsibility to set boundaries and administer discipline according to their developmental stage. Teaching about God's design for them as man or woman will provide them with a biblical framework for life. Helping them to understand the importance of purity and how to deal with social media and various other kinds of temptation will fortify them and provide a solid bulwark to keep them for a life of service. Parenting isn't static—it's a dynamic process. Parents have been given a stewardship and privilege to guide their child and to be purposeful about instilling characteristics at the right time to foster growth in character. Equipping children to make wise decisions and instilling in them a sense of integrity and responsibility will be the capstone for them to live out their ultimate true fulfilment in Christ.

The Life Cycle of Parenting

As a child encounters various challenges and opportunities, his or her character is slowly formed. From the very beginning, the tendency for many doting parents is to overindulge their child, especially their firstborn or perhaps also the youngest. If we pamper our children, however, and permit them to get their way all (or even most of) the time, we inevitably reap the consequences in the form of a spoiled, ungrateful child programmed for getting his or her way. We're unintentionally training a manipulator where the child, rather than the parent, takes charge, the very opposite of fostering the character traits of submission and cooperation in the family. The stewardship is great, not only for our and our children's sake, but also for the sake of family dynamics and unity, the community, and the mission of God. Therefore, it's important to stand firm as parents and to make sure *we're* parenting our *children* rather than *them* parenting *us*.

For this reason, we recommend that, as a parent, you find ways from the beginning of communicating that you, rather than your child, are in charge. This isn't a matter of trying to stifle our children's development and self-expression, or for parents to become overbearing despots. Rather, it's a sign of true, committed love, and a fulfilling of a responsible trust. As the book of Proverbs repeatedly reminds us, discipline is vital in child-rearing, and the loving parent is the one who is there to provide consistent correction and accountability (Prov. 6:23;

12:1; 14:24; 29:15 cf. Eph. 6:4; Heb. 12:5-6, 11; Rev. 3:19). So, as you move through the life cycle of parenting, from infancy to childhood to adolescence and early adulthood, the nature of your relationship with your child will change, but your commitment to building character should be constant. This is what we mean by 'responsibility' in parenting. In the short run, a laissez-faire approach to parenting may seem easier and may be smoother because there may be less conflict— but remember, *your primary goal in parenting is not to minimize conflict but rather to build genuine character.*

So, as your child begins school, is your main goal to see your son or daughter get good grades? Good grades have some value and may be an indication of intelligence and academic ability, or at least of being able to do well within a given system of expectations, but they're not always a reliable indicator of character.

If not grades, is your focus as parents to promote your child's athletic success? Being a good sports parent is one of the signs of a good parent this generation is fixated on. Are you pushing them hard to excel in baseball or basketball or some other sport? You're the perfect soccer parent, present at every game, perhaps even coaching your son's or daughter's team. You sacrifice much of your time, especially on weekends, to invest in your child's recreational pursuits, and take great pains to capture every point scored, every heat won, every home run on camera. Yet your child's heart may be unregenerate, his mind set on winning at all cost, his sense of identity staked on how well he does on the baseball court or football field. In the end, who is going to watch all those videos? What does it matter if your son's team won or lost a given game? But his character will have been formed, for better or for worse, and you won't be able to turn back the clock.

Developing Character

Rather than focusing on good grades or athletic success, invest the bulk of your efforts in helping your child to develop character. What do we mean by 'character'? Essentially, *character* is who a person truly is in their heart, exemplified in what they do when no one's looking. Character means *integrity*, a stable core of *conviction* that isn't easily shaken by peer pressure, cultural influences, or varying circumstances. It is constant.

As you seek to shape your child's character, which values will you wish to impart? Is it serving God, loving others, developing courage, and standing up for what they believe? If so, what will your strategy be to teach and reinforce those values? Character isn't formed by default or by chance. What's more, children tend to imitate their parents' behavior, so we'll want to make sure that we ourselves are people of integrity.

How do we accomplish this? First, we must acknowledge we can't develop character in our children unaided by the Holy Spirit. The burden is beyond measure; we can't do this work in our own strength. The Spirit must do His work in our children as they enter their own relationship with God, striving and aspiring *themselves* to be men and women of integrity and moral excellence.

Paul encourages believers to 'walk by the Spirit' and be 'led by the Spirit' and goes on to write that 'the fruit of the Spirit is love, joy, peace, patience, kindness, goodness, faithfulness, gentleness, self-control' (Gal. 5:16, 18, 22-23). He adds, 'If we live by the Spirit, let us also keep in step with the Spirit' (Gal. 5:24). Elsewhere, he urges believers to be 'filled with the Spirit' (Eph. 5:18). Yet in another place, he writes that 'those who live according to the Spirit set their minds on the things of the Spirit' and adds, 'If the Spirit of him who raised Jesus from the dead dwells in you, he who raised Christ Jesus from the dead will also give life to your mortal bodies through his Spirit who dwells in you' (Rom. 8:5, 11).

What this catena of Scripture passages on the Spirit shows is that it is He who produces in us what is pleasing to God.

As we *walk* with Him, are *led* by Him, *live* in Him, *keep in step* with Him, and are *filled* with Him, we'll set our mind on spiritual things, and the Spirit of the risen Christ will infuse our mortal bodies with supernatural strength to surmount our sinful nature. In this way, we'll be able to please God and do all things through Him who strengthens us (Phil. 4:13). As Paul writes to the Corinthians, 'All things are lawful, but not all things are helpful' (1 Cor. 10:23). Again, the apostle strikes the balance beautifully when he urges believers, 'Work out your own salvation with fear and trembling, for it is God who works in you, both to will and to work for his good pleasure' (Phil. 2:12-13).

Our children should be encouraged to actively 'work out their salvation,' trusting that God is at work in them, both to have the resolute will and the actual ability to live the life God wants them to live. This is true for us as adults, too, and it applies in the same way to our children. If you have successfully introduced your child to Christ, or they have received Him and become a child of God, their spiritual lives can be nurtured by teaching them from Scripture about the work of the Spirit along the lines of the above-cited passages. The last thing we'll want to condition our children to do is live the Christian life in their own strength. This will only lead to failure and frustration, if not despair.

Instilling Virtues

In large part, helping our children develop character entails inculcating *virtues* in them. To break down the matter in more practical terms, children's sinfulness is borne out in several ways: they typically lack self-control and lose their temper, tend to be disobedient (or at least, shall we say, have a mind of their own, redefining the terms of parental instruction), may be lazy and lack a proper work ethic, and are undiscerning and naïve, if not downright foolish, like we once were (if we're honest). If you want more specifics, work through this list from Proverbs. It was written to instruct young men, but the principles apply to boys and girls alike. Here are virtues parents should seek to instill in their young children so that when they're old they will not depart from them (adapted from my book *God, Marriage, and Family*):

- Diligence and industriousness (6:6-11; 11:27; 12:24; 13:4; 15:19; 18:9; 19:24; 20:4, 13; 21:5; 22:13; 26:13-16)

- Justice (11:1; 16:11; 17:23; 20:10, 23; 31:8-9)

- Kindness (11:17)

- Generosity (11:24; 19:6)

- Self-control, particularly of speech (12:18; 13:3; 21:23) and temper (14:17, 29; 15:18; 16:32; 19:11; see also 25:28)

- Righteousness (12:21, 28; 14:34)

- Truthfulness and honesty (12:22; 16:13; 24:26)

- Discretion in choosing friends (13:20; 18:24), particularly a spouse (18:22; 31:10-31)

- Caution and prudence (14:16; 27:12)

- Gentleness (15:1, 4)

- Contentment (15:16-17; 16:8; 17:1)

- Integrity of character (15:27; 28:18)

- Humility (16:19; 18:12; 22:4)

- Graciousness (16:24)

- Forthrightness (rather than duplicity; 16:30; 17:20)

- Restraint (17:14, 27-28; 18:6-7; 29:20)

- Faithfulness in friendship (17:17) and otherwise (28:20)

- Purity (20:9; 22:11)

- Vigorous pursuit of what is good and right (20:29)

- Skillfulness in work (22:29)

- Patience (25:15)

How do you go about instilling these virtues in your children? Start with yourself. You must put a priority on developing character. You can even verbalize this by telling your children that while you rejoice in their prowess at basketball or ballet, even winning and achieving, you value even more their integrity in dealing with others (e.g. 'I liked how you encouraged the other players and didn't brag about yourself'). After a while, it may come about that they value what you value because they innately want to please you and tend to imitate and emulate your values.

Humility

Let's look at the virtue that is the foundation of all the other virtues. The world's definition of greatness is vastly different from God's.

Watch any basketball game on TV, and you'll be treated to a never-ending series of wild, chest-beating celebrations of virtually every single basket scored. One might think those players just accomplished an unprecedented feat of courage or some other rare achievement when, in fact, they merely scored a basket worth 2 points (or maybe 3).

Over against such inflated conceptions of greatness is the biblical definition of true greatness in God's eyes. In a key passage, Yahweh (the LORD) states: 'This is the one I will esteem: he who is humble and contrite in spirit, who trembles at My word' (Isa. 66:2 BSB). Conversely, the root sin in Lucifer's heart prior to his fall from grace was that of pride: 'How you are fallen from heaven, O Day Star, son of Dawn! ... You said in your heart, "I will ascend to heaven; above the stars of God I will set my throne on high ...; I will make myself like the Most High"' (Isa. 14:12-14).

In the Gospels, Jesus affirmed that 'even the Son of Man [Jesus Himself] came not to be served but to serve and to give his life as a ransom [sacrifice] for many' (Mark 10:45). In a similar vein, James cites an Old Testament proverb: 'God opposes the proud but gives grace to the humble' (James 4:6; Prov. 3:34). What these verses show is that the humble person does not exalt himself over others or even God but deflects any glory for himself to God and others in recognition of his dependence on Him and them.

Where, you may ask, can true greatness be found in a person? The greatest example is *Jesus*, 'who, though he was in the form of God, did not count equality with God a thing to be grasped, but emptied himself by taking the form of a servant, being born in the likeness of men. And being found in human form, he humbled himself by becoming obedient to the point of death, even death on a cross. Therefore God has highly exalted him ...' (Phil. 2:6-9; John 13:1-20).

Other such people may include one's *parents*, certain people in our *church*, and other *unsung heroes* and *selfless servants*, people exhibiting qualities or engaging in acts that are genuinely sacrificial, humble, and unselfish. Luke tells the story of Jesus perceiving such an unselfish act during His earthly ministry: 'And he looked up and saw the rich putting their gifts into the treasury. And he saw a poor widow putting in two small copper coins. And he said, "Truly I say to you, this poor widow put in more than all of them; for they all out of their surplus put into the offering; but she out of her poverty put in all that she had to live on"' (Luke 21:1-4 NASB). It's truly mind-transforming to ponder that a small and humble gesture can be considered great in the eyes of God. Astounding!

Parental Ambitions and Aspirations

Applied to parenting, ask yourself: What are my ambitions for my children? Are these in keeping with God's definition of greatness? How are you preparing and mentoring your children to move them in a Godward direction? Are you more focused on temporary recognitions or eternal rewards? We already mentioned the danger of pampering our children. What's the proper balance between loving your children and making them feel special yet not idolizing them? Virtually all parents are proud of their children's accomplishments—just look at your preferred social media site! Chances are, it's full of proud parents 'humbly' parading the accomplishments of their children.

Our own aspiration in this regard is threefold:

- **Try not to brag.** There are proper ways to acknowledge publicly how proud you are of your child, but we might aim to do this in as understated and humble a way as possible. In this way, we won't arouse the jealousy of others. Also, we won't inflate our child's sense of self-importance. We can certainly be grateful in our hearts to God for allowing our child to reach a milestone and tell our child privately how proud we are of them. Of course, we'll want to make sure they know that our love for them is not conditioned by their successes or failures but that we love them no matter what. I sometimes tell my son before a game that even if he scores zero points, I'll love him just the same, so he knows not to connect my love for him to his performance.

- **Don't overdo special occasions.** Birthdays, for example, are special occasions, but in the overall scheme are really not that important. Another year has passed. This doesn't mark an accomplishment but simply the passage of time. I think we're often too fixated on marking special occasions, and this at times becomes a burden, an expectation to live up to, especially with multiple children. It's almost as if birthday parties are considered a measure of whether and how much you love your kids these days! Focusing on special occasions may also perpetuate an undue emphasis on events and gifts, proportionately lessening the amount of attention we give to less easily qualifiable matters such as character development. Now please don't get us wrong here: Of course, it's great to have times when you can make people feel special and loved on their birthday. We just want to guard against any excesses here. In our experience, it's easy to go over the top. By all means, let's make our children feel special, but let's not idolize them or cause them to stumble.

- **Encourage excellence.** As parents, we should try to inculcate in our children a *commitment to excellence*—to strive to excel in whatever it is they're doing. This may mean refraining from investing undue effort in certain sports or musical instruments in which they have no or little natural gifting while directing most of their energies on activities in which they stand out among their peers. Try to find out what your child is good at and then encourage them to develop those skills to the fullest over time.

Work Ethic

Does your child tend to be lazy? Most of us must work for a living, so for this reason at the very least (besides the value of responsible work for beauty in character) it's an important part of parenting to instill in our children a proper *work ethic*. One important principle here is that work comes before pleasure. Put differently, responsibility comes before privilege.

Does he want to watch a show or go out for ice cream? Well, has he done his homework or chores? This seems obvious but needs constant reinforcing.

It's also important to convey that none of us always feels like doing certain tasks, even though they must be done. Did I feel like spending a portion of my Saturday afternoon mowing the lawn? Hardly—but it needed to be done, so I did it.

The same is true for them: Just do your geometry homework, if for no other reason than that it is due tomorrow.

It's particularly vital to stress the importance of developing good study habits and a solid work ethic while our children are young because it is at this stage that they'll form habits that will stay with them for the rest of their lives.

Wisdom and Discernment

Does your child lack *discernment*? Do they say 'yes' when their peers ask them to join them in doing something that turns out to be foolish and gets them into trouble? As a parent, engage your child's reasoning process, so that you can see how he or she thinks through an issue. Then, try to instill practical decision-making skills by helping them to ask questions such as:

- **Why do I want to do this?** This will get at their underlying motivation: Is it to please people? Is it to get instant gratification? Or is it truly a wise course of action that will benefit them and others and bring glory to God?

- **What will happen when I decide to do this?** Help them to anticipate unintended consequences of their decisions, especially negative ones.

- **What are my alternatives?** This will help them to weigh the pros and cons of a given decision and help them realize that often decisions are not black and white: There may be advantages and disadvantages to most courses of action, so the best decisions are those that weigh the pros and cons and choose the best alternative.

- **What do people I trust recommend?** It's usually wise to consult with others, and to ask not just one's peers but those who are wiser and more experienced, such as one's parents or other trusted individuals such as teachers, counselors, pastors, or youth leaders.

Practical Decision-Making Principles

	Principle	Brief Description
1	Why do I want to do this?	Search your heart to examine your motives
2	What will happen when I decide to do this?	Determine positive or negative consequences of making a given decision
3	What are my alternatives?	If possible, make a list of all the possible available choices
4	What do people I trust recommend?	Determine if there is a coalescing consensus among trusted counselors

We've been at this with our children for many years now and have found that equipping them to make sensible, mature, and discerning decisions is one of the most important long-term goals we should adopt as parents.

Dealing with Adversity

One of the major ways in which character is formed is by dealing with various kinds of adversity. If we encounter an obstacle or things don't go our way, our natural—sinful—tendency is to whine and pout like the Israelites in the wilderness! Most of us live in unbelievable luxury compared with much of the world population, and what do we do? We whine and complain! We've found that one of the main challenges of parenting is to teach our children genuine gratitude. Better still is to embrace adversity that God allows in their lives as opportunities to develop Christlike character. A true believer is yielded to God's will being done in their lives, whether this confounds their own well-laid plans or not (Prov. 16:9). God never promised us that life would be easy and that we'd always get our way.

Again, let's make sure that we first take this truth to heart ourselves. If I get mad when someone cuts me off in traffic when my sons are in the car with me, I shouldn't be surprised if they get mad when the umpire calls them 'Out!' when they were safe on base. I still vividly remember visiting with an American missionary family in Madrid, Spain, when my friend lost his way badly in busy traffic.

Rather than give him a tough time, his wife was very sweet and supportive and affirmed and encouraged him; and you can be sure the children noticed. What a wonderful role model of handling adversity in a Christlike manner! That event took place decades ago, but I still remember it because it showed a demeanor that went counter to our natural, sinful tendency to complain when something goes wrong.

Self-control

Does your child frequently lose his temper? Again, first ask yourself: Are you yourself exemplifying self-control in demanding situations? Talk to your child about the importance of self-control and find ways to help him grow in this area. To some extent, emotional stability increases with age, but we should start early in helping our children develop self-control. When studying Paul's letters to Timothy and Titus, I was amazed to discover that the one constant quality Paul's apostolic delegates were consistently told to engender in various groups in their congregation—older men, young men, older women, young women—is self-control (Titus 2:2, 5, 6, 12). Self-control is also the ninth and final fruit of the Spirit (Gal. 5:23).

Work with your children on dealing with adversity and controlling their temper. Affirm them when they take baby steps toward accepting a 'no' answer to their request to stay up late or to have brownies for breakfast. Make sure they're secure in your and God's love, so they know it's not the end of the world if they drop a ball or mess up on their recital piece. As one of our son's baseball coaches would repeat *ad nauseam*, 'Process, not results.' If you work hard on the process, results will come. We're all growing and developing in different areas, so let's help our children to set reasonable expectations for themselves and to experience success in meeting them, gradually setting the bar higher until they excel by God's grace and patience and self-control are increasingly built into their character.

Preparing Your Children for Mission

Protective parents will try to shield their children from the evils of the surrounding culture in a well-intentioned effort to spare them unnecessary harm, defilement, or moral compromise. Parents certainly have a vital responsibility to protect their children from negative influences, especially during the early years when they are more impressionable and vulnerable, and their character is still being formed. A long-term perspective on parenting, however, includes equipping our children to engage people in the surrounding culture with the gospel message.

Just as Jesus gathered a circle of close followers around him for a few years, trained them in ministry, and then sent them out on mission in the world, we, too, should be diligent and take time to build up and train our children—not just to keep the gospel to themselves and keep out of harm's way. As parents our aim should be to equip our children so they can be salt and light in their sphere of influence, something they won't be able to do if they always keep others at arm's length and fail to get involved (Matt. 5:13-16).

Set Apart for God	→	**Sanctify**	→	**Send Out**
(Past Event)		(Process)		(Goal)

Before commissioning His followers, Jesus prayed for them to the Father: 'Sanctify them in your truth; your word is truth' (John 17:17). God had called them and set them apart; now the Holy Spirit must do His sanctifying work in them so they are ready for God to use them as His witnesses. Then they would be sent out (John 17:18; 20:21-22). Therefore, encourage your child to go through the process of growing in the truth of God's Word *before* they're sent out. In our home, we've found that our children began to be ready for these kinds of conversations and cultural involvement in their early to mid-teens (varying from child to child). They started asking questions, and their character began to take shape as they had to make moral choices that set them apart from their peers.

There are two opposite dangers with which parents are faced in equipping and sending out their children into the world. On the one hand is the danger of sending out your children too early, underestimating the challenges they may face. As a result, we may feed them to the lions of the culture who may devour them because they're insufficiently prepared to stand firm when they face the strong headwinds of the culture. On the other hand is the opposite danger of undue delaying or never sending our children out at all, whether out of fear or out of a lack of missions-mindedness. Such parents fail to recognize that we're put on this earth to be God's witnesses; they enjoy His good gifts (pre-eminently His salvation in Christ) for themselves but never share it with others who desperately need it.

So, then, *first*, equip your children thoroughly and responsibly with biblical truth, and make sure they're solid in character, growing in Christ, and discerning. Only *then* send them out, filled with the Spirit and part of a believing community, when you prayerfully determine they're ready. They certainly shouldn't try to go it alone but serve in company with like-minded others. In this way, they'll be accountable to those who can provide a support network and partner with them in being on mission for and with God. It's been our joy to see several young men and women who have been equipped and are now serving on university campuses or on the mission field, being powerfully used by God.

Dealing with Technology and Social Media

One primary way in which character, specifically self-control, is revealed and shaped in our children is through social media. Modern technology and social media are one important reason why many parents feel that raising children is more complicated today than it has been in the past. Yet this is not only a problem for young people; many of us parents do not have this area of our lives under control either, spending far more time on the internet than is healthy. What does this mean for the impressionable thirteen-year-old seeking new and exciting pastimes? In our experience we have found that youth don't normally have the self-control and wisdom to deal with this area unaided by their parents. To address the challenges faced related to social media, two considerations are paramount: first, primarily *character*, that stems from the heart of the child; and second, the need for setting appropriate *boundaries* including *accountability*.

During the teenage years, character continues to be formed, peer pressure is high, and values and convictions are being sharpened in the crucible of a harsh world. Self-control—such as for boys when it comes to sexually explicit images and pornography—may vary depending on circumstances. As Jesus told His followers, 'The spirit is willing, but the flesh is weak' (Matt. 26:41 NIV). That assumes we have the best of intentions! Even so, our human makeup is tenuous and fragile. There'll be times when vulnerability and susceptibility to temptation is more acute than others, such as on evenings during downtime or when tired and defenses are down.

Talk to your children about these things to make sure that they begin to develop a lifetime of holy living in a challenging world. Knowing themselves well and being astute to the potential vulnerable aspects also of their circumstances (living, work, or school), will help them to continually adjust and set proper boundaries, guarding against temptation in the complexities of life. In setting boundaries for social media, good stewardship of time is vital. You can still affirm the positive potential for connectedness and relationship, even ministry, but expressing caution and urging wisdom and discernment is crucial! Embrace the opportunity to discuss this with your son or daughter. Ideally, they'll *want* to set boundaries themselves and will *own* these boundaries rather than having such merely imposed on them by their parents. Again, this is not a question of character *vs.* boundaries, but rather one of both character *and* boundaries! Putting certain controls and restrictions in place is an example of the biblical principle of *not making provision for the flesh* (Rom. 13:14).

Another important principle is that of *accountability*. In the case of younger children, we should make sure we know their passwords and have unlimited access to their social media platforms, not only to keep them accountable but also to protect them from sexual predators. It goes without saying that we should set the example in this area and ourselves seek appropriate accountability and put a high priority on guarding our own moral purity, especially in our social media and internet usage. It may help to be appropriately vulnerable and transparent with our son or daughter about any issues we've faced in this regard as well. This will encourage them and strengthen our bond with them further. They need to know that they're not alone, that we're not perfect either, and we'd love to help in any way we can!

On a positive side, the best antidote against excessive social media use or succumbing to temptation on the internet is a strong *love for God*, being busy in *doing the Lord's work* and serving Him with reliance on the *power of the Holy Spirit*. This presupposes that our children have a growing relationship with the Lord and that they're actively nurturing this relationship through being in the Word and prayer. While they're at home with us, we can help them develop such healthy spiritual habits. Even when they're in college, we can continue to keep them accountable and encourage them in their walk with the Lord.

Above all, we should always *keep lines of communication open*— relational parenting! They should feel like they can always talk to us, especially when they need to confess that they may have slipped up in this area. While we should take sin very seriously, we should be thankful that they confide in us and assure them of God's boundless grace and forgiveness. It's amazing when we experience together the truth of John 1:9: 'If we confess our sins, he is faithful and just to forgive our sins and to cleanse us from all unrighteousness.'

The tech-wise family will use technology in its proper place. Social media can be a remarkable tool but shouldn't be an idol or be taken lightly. Help your child to find their identity in Christ, not through social media and approval they find in it—intensely seeking photo-ops to present themselves in a certain light, 'likes' and comments on their posts, etc. Instead, let's extol the preeminent role of spirituality and character in dealing with social media. And let's remember: Character matters—it always does.

Conclusion

It's character, parents! Focus your energies on developing character in your children. Don't worry too much about good grades or athletic achievements. They have their place, but character trumps scholastic or athletic accomplishments in the end because it is a permanent fixture in our lives even unto eternity. Winning a tournament or playing at a recital, on the other hand, is ephemeral—here today, gone tomorrow, usually quickly forgotten. Therefore, parents, care more about inculcating virtues such as integrity, honesty, and selflessness in your children than being preoccupied with or blinded by external badges of honor.

The virtues God celebrates are the fruit of the Spirit—love, joy, peace, patience, kindness, goodness, faithfulness, gentleness, and self-control. If your child were to have to take his or her final exam in these characteristics, how would they do? What grade would they get in self-control, for example? What about the other virtues on the list? And what about you: How would *you* do? We know these are convicting questions. Of course, any progress in these areas is due to the work of God's Spirit within us. Nevertheless, Scripture urges us to 'make every effort' to actively pursue these virtues and to excel in them (2 Pet. 1:3-11).

♦ *Reflect on and discuss what degree of significance you are currently attaching to character development in your children. If you've concluded that you don't devote enough attention to character, what do you need to do to revisit your priorities and to make character development a priority?*

♦ *How are your children dealing with adversity in their lives, such as when they are not getting their way? Do they blame others? And, how are you dealing with adversity? Are you setting a good example in this regard, and what can you do to help your children improve in this area?*

♦ *How do you go about encouraging your children to be humble? Are you setting a good example in this regard? What's the difference between aiming high and trying to excel, and being boastful or prideful in one's pursuit of or admiration of 'greatness'? Think of concrete ways in which you could improve, whether in sports, school, or other areas.*

8

Education

While character trumps education in parenting, education is also very important! Parents should affirm their ultimate responsibility for their children's education, selecting schooling options wisely, and considering the unusual spiritual and other benefits of schooling children at home.

♦ *Read Psalm 119:9-11. What does this passage tell you about the importance of young people being immersed in God's Word and allowing it to shape their hearts?*

♦ *Read 2 Timothy 3:14-17. What does this passage tell you about the importance of the Scriptures in a child's upbringing as well as about the role of parents and godly mentors?*

Education is an all-encompassing part of our children's lives. For this reason, we believe it best to approach education as a natural process rather than compartmentalizing it. An important dimension of parenting is passing on our spiritual and cultural heritage to our children. This may include language learning, family history, travel, music and instruments, communication skills (interpersonal and public), and teaching social and etiquette skills. Educating our offspring also involves learning how to teach gifted or developmentally challenged children (if you have a child in either or both categories), determining our child's learning style, and practicing the most effective methods of learning. We also have the privilege of helping our children learn how to make and save money and even how to handle their sexual urges and wait for sex until marriage. Educating our children is exceedingly important, and as parents we shouldn't want to surrender this incredible opportunity for impact and influence to anyone else.

The Value of Education

While, as mentioned, we feel strongly about the priority of developing character, we value education in our family a great deal. We want our children to learn about *both* God's *Word* and God's *world*. The way this is evident is in the fact that we allocate significant resources to education, both in terms of time and energy, and in terms of finance. It is our desire that each of our children eventually go to any university regardless of cost if that is where God leads. We've decided to trust God to provide the necessary funds if one of our children really feels drawn to a school and we believe that, all things considered, this is the best place for them to go.

Why is education so important to us? We believe that it provides a solid foundation for a lifetime of contributing to God's world and to God's mission. We also believe that education elevates a person by imparting knowledge and expertise in a field of study and, beyond this, teaches critical thinking and research skills that they can apply to every area of life. For example, I never worked directly in my original field of economics but acquired valuable research, writing, and marketing skills during my studies that have frequently proven helpful. In addition, we believe getting a quality education is also good stewardship of resources and time.

How are your children spending their time and resources? All things being equal (the job market is not always predictable), our children will be better able to use their gifting and achieve their potential in appropriate vocations if they have a good education. This will help them—especially our boys as leaders—to serve God and support their family well. Getting the best possible education is also in keeping with the virtue of excellence, enabling a person to use their talents in a field of study and line of work. To be sure, some skills can be self-taught, but overall, we're firm believers in the value of formal education at their level, where students draw on the comprehensive body of knowledge in a field rather than trying to figure things out inductively. Very often in life, problems arise when a person attempts to tackle a task in which they're insufficiently trained. There's no substitute for formal education from experts in the field.

When it comes to vocational preparation, therefore, we don't believe in cutting corners. We discourage our children from going the easy way, the path of least resistance, just to get any degree. Nor should lack of finances ultimately dictate our educational choices. For one, it's not just, or even primarily, about getting a *degree*—it's about learning a given subject matter well and being equipped for life by acquiring *expertise* so you can pursue excellence. Mediocrity rarely glorifies God or serves other people well—*excellence* does. So don't just substitute your hard classes in college by taking an easier equivalent at the local community college, even if that's what all your friends are doing. Prayerfully, help your child balance the demands in their lives, but encourage them to aspire to the harder thing if possible, realizing that some classes may be challenging, but if they enroll in them, and persist, they'll learn a great deal that they'll be able to use for the rest of their life.

School Choice

So what's the right way to school your children? What's the best way for them to begin learning about God's world and developing personal expertise to contribute to God's mission? While some may believe that the answer is universal—whether schooling at home, Christian private school, or public school education—our experience suggests that the answer to this question depends on a variety of factors and may even vary for each child, and even from one year to another. We firmly believe in the importance of school choice, and certainly, as parents, we should talk and pray long and hard about where to have our children schooled. When it comes to education, we believe one size doesn't fit all.

We can share a little bit of our experience here; others will be able to give different input. To begin with, depending on the legal situation in your country or state, we encourage you to consider *schooling your children at home*. We've schooled all our children at home with occasional exceptions. We're both educators, and certainly want what's best for them. Since God supplied us with the means to do so, we chose to educate our children ourselves, which was enriching for us as parents and has been a great joy. We found like-minded parents and families supporting each other; a community that shared resources, skills, and spiritual encouragement amongst themselves.

Though at first, it was an intimidating choice, we believe it was the most important choice we made when it comes to parenting our children. Many questions confronted us—would we be up to the task of schooling multiple children at the same time, teaching them different subjects on various levels of education? What curriculum would we use? What about our children's social life and interaction with others? Would they all become social misfits? And what about science (we have no chemistry lab), music, sports, and other electives?

The first few years we attended a conference where we received invaluable input from experienced parents including being introduced to organizations that serve parents who school their children at home. We gleaned many practical tips, such as how to put together a high school curriculum, how to prepare a transcript for college applications, how to best prepare our children for college admission tests, and how to get legal advice and protection if needed.

We found several advantages to schooling at home. First, schooling children at home provided an amazing and close *bond* between us parents and the children, and even among siblings. We consider it a privilege to have guided and educated our own children primarily from home and to have built upon shared experiences, taking advantage of opportunities to shape character along the way. Of course, you may not always have the necessary skills or knowledge yourself to teach a given subject but praise the Lord for competent science teachers (with labs in their homes!) and co-ops with qualified teachers who can help share the load. My wife would typically handle the core subjects—math, English, science, and history—while I would take responsibility for the electives: languages, sports, and music. Also,

I would typically prepare my children for the college admissions test and help them with their applications.

Second, you can *tailor* the education to a child's interests, abilities, and learning styles. Some of your children may be more academically inclined than others who are more practically oriented. You may have a particularly gifted child, a child that takes longer to grasp a given context, or a developmentally challenged child. If you school your children at home, you can go at your child's pace and adapt your instruction to the way your children learn best.

Third, you have added control over your child's *curriculum*. You don't have to teach them evolution or the 'virtues' of same-sex marriage or transgender. You can teach your classes from a Christian worldview perspective. You can even add overtly Christian electives such as apologetics (defending your faith) or hermeneutics (how to study the Bible). You can also choose a curriculum that integrates multiple subjects, such as English literature, world history, and Bible. You can include subjects not always taught in public or other schools, such as speech and debate, logic or Latin. In our family, we've greatly enjoyed our children taking part in several speech and debate tournaments, and my husband has taught Latin to a small group of children—including our own—in our home.

Fourth, you have additional *flexibility*, which is especially helpful if you, like us, can travel and minister at various places during the year. In addition, you can use your travels for education purposes (field trips!). Over the years, we've traveled through much of North America and part of Europe, which in large part was possible because of added flexibility through schooling at home. Occasional field trips (local as well) are invaluable because they provide real-life encounters and show the relevance of what our children are learning in the home classroom. In keeping education interesting, field trips can make an enormous difference though we understand it may not always be economically or otherwise feasible for families to travel all over the world.

We could go on to list further advantages of schooling children at home, but as you can see, whether you're able or find it advantageous to do so or not, there are many reasons why you might want to consider assuming the responsibility for the education of your children. In your role as a parent, if you choose to entrust the care or education of your children to someone else, make sure their values match your own as closely as possible, or you'll have to undo some of the negative influences that will likely ensue. Schooling at home is not for everyone, of course. Start thinking early about what your values are regarding your children's education and how to best ensure that they carry the day. Unless you're *intentional* about your children's education, someone else—often with values different than your own—will call the shots, and you may not always like the results.

Benefits of Schooling Children at Home

	Benefit	Brief Description
1	Create a close bond between parent and child, siblings	Spend invaluable time with child teaching them subjects in area of own expertise
2	Tailor education to individual interests, abilities, and learning styles	Greater individual attention, more effective education
3	Control over curriculum	Offer subjects not taught at public school, classical curriculum, values, Bible, etc.
4	Flexibility	Opportunity for field trips, extracurricular educational opportunities, travel

Responsible parents will make every effort to make an informed and prayerful decision regarding their children's education. Find out what your options are. Realize that what may be right for one child may not be best for another. We've always taken it one year at a time, one child at a time though our preference was to coordinate all the children's schooling. Also, while we believe that educating our children from home was the most strategic parenting choice we made, we know that there are circumstances that lend themselves to other school options for a given family: public school, Christian private school, or some other arrangement (but, remember, you'll be giving up a good deal of parental presence, authority, and protection in those cases). It's up to you to determine what to do in any given year with a given child, keeping in mind the larger foundational values that should guide your decision-making regarding your child's schooling. Also, the educational scene (including the legal situation) will vary depending on the country, state, or educational district where you live.

Life Experiences as Education

Education is more than just head knowledge acquired from books, or at school. It's all-round preparation for life—learning about personal giftedness and finding one's place in God's world. This includes academics but should also involve real-life experience gained working with other people and serving in the community. If you school from home, this is more easily and thoroughly incorporated in your days together.

A significant part of parenting is passing on our spiritual and cultural heritage to our children. While we don't have the space to go into detail here, let us just mention some of the necessary ingredients in the educational mix you'll likely want to provide for your children, whether you school from home or elsewhere, including some tips on preparing for college admission.

First, know what the minimal requirements are for your state (or country). Determine if your child is likely to be on track toward college and if so, learn what the general college requirements are, as well as those for specific universities they may aspire to attend. Requirements vary. You also need to know your child and their personal and academic bent. Guide them individually here.

In addition to covering core courses for your children's education, you'll want to encourage them to learn one or several *foreign languages*. Of course, make sure you start with teaching them your native language well, such as English for most of you reading this book. Too often we've found that young people are weak in the basics of grammar and syntax (sentence structure). There are so many benefits to learning another language and traveling to other countries. Your children's heart for others will be stirred and their horizons expanded. They'll see their own lives in larger perspective and will be able to relate better to people who are different than them. Learning a foreign language will reinforce their grasp of their own native language. They'll be able to read works written in another language and communicate with people in other cultures. Even if they can't *speak* the language, they'll still appreciate other customs and people—their musical styles, special dishes, etc.

Not only does education include language learning, it may also include mastering a *musical instrument*. Whether you're gifted musically or not, most of us enjoy listening to music and have distinct tastes and preferences in musical style. In addition, some of our children may have special musical abilities; we should encourage them to develop those for the glory of God and the enjoyment of us all. In fact, it's not just being able to play an instrument that is worth pursuing; one thing I, as a parent, appreciate is the character formation that accompanies taking music lessons. Over time, a young person acquires a certain amount of discipline by having weekly music lessons and by practicing pieces on a daily (or almost daily) basis. Music education is a gift for all students. It can also be a lot of fun to play in an orchestra or a band and to see how one can make beautiful music together with others.

The same benefit of discipline can come from playing *sports*. In our family, we've been greatly blessed with basketball coaches who viewed sports as a means of discipleship. Some matched up more mature players with less mature ones as 'accountability partners' as part of a mentoring program. Others hosted regular Bible studies and prayer times. These coaches challenged those young players not to wait until after college to take an interest in spiritual things but to accept responsibility for becoming a strong Christian while they're young. In an age when we too often pamper our children, we appreciate coaches who are rigorous in terms of physical discipline as well as in spiritual accountability. Not that we should delegate this role entirely to a coach or teacher, but it surely helps to partner with coaches, other parents, and role models who can be allies with us in mentoring and discipling our children.

Regarding your *spiritual heritage*, make sure to tell your children how you came to know the Lord. Share your testimony with them! Show them where you grew up and tell them about some of the things you did as a young person and how and when and where you met the Lord.

Part of their education and socialization is also to teach them about their *family history* and *ethnic and cultural heritage*. Share about family traditions and some of their ancestors. You could even engage in genealogical family research together.

Also, put special emphasis on helping your children develop strong public and private *communication* and *interpersonal skills*. This will be aided by reading and developing an active vocabulary. It'll also be enhanced by participating in an informal or formal speech and debate program. Teaching your children social skills and etiquette, in a way that helps them to act with kindness toward those around them, will be beneficial to them and anyone they meet.

We talked about the 'Big Three'—money, sex, and in-laws. Don't wait until pre-marital counseling to tackle these vital topics. Some parents are rather secretive about their *finances* (others are just disorganized). Try to find appropriate, and if necessary discreet ways to draw your children into the way in which you manage your money and to mentor them in these areas. You may establish a budget organized by categories (housing, food, clothing, education, entertainment, etc.) and share it with your children. This will help teach them the value—and limited availability—of money and to be more appreciative for the way in which God provides for your family. Also, you'll probably want to start them on an age-appropriate allowance. As they grow older, you can encourage them to find part-time employment locally. Help guide them in making wise decisions on how to spend their money allowing them gradually to make their own choices. They'll learn from their successes and failures. Later still, you can help them research how to invest their money and guide them in their financial decision-making.

Make yourself available to teach them about *sex*. Delegating sex education to others, such as the public school, is a questionable decision for any Christian parent. So, you must take initiative in your home to set the stage for their lives in these ways. Sex is one of God's most extraordinary gifts, to be enjoyed exclusively in marriage. Prepare your child beforehand for these kinds of talks from others. We've found that the age of twelve is generally an appropriate time to do this, before children enter the teenage years. That said, if you try to initiate conversation and your child is disinterested, you may want to wait until he or she is ready. Alternatively, if they're asking questions earlier, take the opportunity to talk about the subject at the level at which your child is interested and ready to address it. In a nonjudgmental way, make sure they know they can always come to you and talk to you about their struggles in this area. Be personal and share (appropriately) some of your own struggles with them and offer advice on how to guard against succumbing to sexual temptation. We continue to pray that God will guide our children to pursue relationships that honor him.

Conclusion

Within the context of character development, place considerable value on your child's education. Education is very crucial, though not all-important! Be responsible as a parent in this crucial area of your child's life. Establish spiritual and educational values and goals and choose the most appropriate form of education for each of your children at every juncture of their development. As you do so, there is freedom to partner with others but assume ultimate responsibility for their education. As your children grow older, involve them increasingly in this decision-making process as part of equipping them for life.

♦ *How important is your child's education for you? And what type of school do you prefer: public school, private school, schooling at home, or some other setting, and why? Are there circumstances such as finances or expediency that influence your choice?*

♦ *Has this chapter affected your view on what education is and how you can best fulfill your role as a parent concerning your children's education? Do you believe parents' spiritual duty to educate their children is part of fulfilling their role as parents?*

♦ *How can you increase your education-mindedness in your family? How can you inspire in your children a greater joy of learning and discovery? How can you genuinely accept responsibility for your children's education regardless of the type of school you choose?*

9
Mission

Parenting takes place at the intersection of three missions that encompass the
parent, the child, and ultimately God. The mission of parenting—bringing
children into this world and raising them to love and serve God—involves
equipping children for their particular mission in life and takes place within
the larger scope of the mission of God: raising up a people who love and
serve Him for His glory. As parents help their children find their place in
this world, they can assist them in determining their natural and spiritual
gifting, guide them in pursuing a potential career/calling, and aid them in
charting a wise course of action in life and significant relationships.

♦ *Read Romans 12:1–2. What can you learn from*
  this passage about decision-making and the will of
  God in a person's life?

♦ *Read Ephesians 5:18, 21–33. How can you teach*
  your children about the distinctive roles of husband
  and wife as you prepare them for marriage?

One of the most exciting privileges of parenting is helping guide our
children toward their mission in life. As parents help their children
discern their calling from God and discover their natural and spiritual
gifts, the children can learn to serve the Lord in their church and move
toward choosing a life vocation. Helping them in this way requires a
listening approach to your child and to God. What are your children's

strengths? What is the best way for them to pursue their calling? How should they go about choosing a life partner? How do we guide them to discern God's will for their lives?

The Mission of God

Rather than focus primarily on God's individual mission for your child—or yourself—it is instructive to start with God's own mission. Once we have a clear picture of God's mission in this world, we'll be able to see more clearly how we each can join God in his mission. So, what is God's mission? This question entails biblical theology, that is, a study of the story line of the Bible to discern God's overall plan. Like a symphony, it is helpful to view the story of Scripture as unfolding in four movements: *Creation*, *Fall*, *Redemption*, and *Consummation*. Within these four movements, consummation corresponds to creation, and redemption corresponds to the Fall.

'In the beginning,' the Bible tells us, 'God *created* the heavens and the earth' (Gen. 1:1). The Bible presupposes God's eternal existence. Those who don't believe in God should contemplate that there is abundant evidence in our world for the existence of a master designer and creator. What's more, not only did God create the heavens and the earth in general, He created you and your children specifically. By getting married and starting a family, you're already fully engaged in God's mission, for the Creator charged the first couple, who had become one flesh in marriage, to multiply and fill the earth. Thus, marriage and family are a central and integral part of God's purposes for humanity generally and for each of us individually.

In exploring God's mission, people in the church often start immediately with the Great Commission which is found at the end of the Gospel of Matthew (28:18-20). The risen Jesus's commissioning of the eleven apostles as *representatives of the church* is indeed a climactic moment in Jesus's mission and vital in understanding His purpose for His *new messianic community, the church*. However, if you *start* there, we believe you're missing some important dimensions and entailments of God's mission in this world that affect you and us very directly. Specifically, you're missing the fact that the Great Commission isn't just addressed to followers of Christ generically but to these followers specifically as *husbands* and *wives* and as *fathers* and *mothers*. Being a Christian will play itself out in community, in teamwork, and in the *local church* by merely living out His design for you as man and woman. In this way, the Great Commission builds on God's original purpose for creating humanity in the first place, extending God's glory throughout the earth as man and woman partner in the procreation of children and thus exercise dominion on His behalf.

At this point in this brief overview, we must introduce the second movement in the biblical story, the *Fall* of humanity. If the Fall hadn't occurred, God's purpose for marriages and offspring would have resulted in families spreading the knowledge of the Creator to the ends of the earth by extending and reflecting His image and likeness throughout the earth. However, the Fall introduced a major complication—to put it mildly—into the divine mandate for humanity. When Eve took of the forbidden fruit and Adam followed suit, the result was that now all of humanity was implicated, and all are now considered to have sinned and fallen short of the glory of God (Rom. 3:23). Think of it as a broken mirror. You can still look at it and see your face, but your facial features will be distorted, and you'll need to get a new, unbroken one, to see the true image. You just can't adequately fix a broken mirror.

Something similar happened to humanity when Adam and Eve transgressed God's command. They could no longer fulfill God's original mandate for them—which wasn't merely to marry and have children (though this continues imperfectly in our world with believers and unbelievers alike), but originally was an institution created to *reflect His image and glory*. Now marriage and family can reflect God only imperfectly, like a broken mirror. In fact, God expelled the first man and woman from His direct, immediate presence in the Garden; so now sinful human beings could no longer live in God's presence but were instead separated from Him. What makes matters worse, there's nothing they (or we) could (can) do to save themselves (ourselves) from this exceedingly serious predicament. With the apostle Paul, we cry, 'Wretched man that I am! Who will deliver me from this body of death?' (Rom. 7:24). Once humanity had rebelled against God, people had become impotent to save themselves and fulfill His mission. The next move was up to God.

And, thank God, he *did* move, albeit very slowly, in what constitutes the third movement in the biblical story. Over the course of Old Testament history, God gradually exposed human sin—especially in the universal flood—and then chose individuals in and through whom He would act *redemptively* in the Messiah. He chose a man named Abram (later renamed Abraham) and promised that in him, through his descendant, all the nations of the earth would be blessed (Gen. 12:1–3). Later, he chose Moses and appointed him to lead His people Israel out of bondage in Egypt and to give them the Law, communicating His specific expectations (the standard of righteousness) in the interim between the Fall and the coming of the Messiah (Exod. 20; Deut. 5). Later still, He chose David to rule His people Israel as a caring shepherd, the forerunner of the Messiah, who would be called the 'Son of David' (2 Sam. 7:13–14). Then, in the 'fullness of time,' God's appointed time, God sent His Son, the Lord Jesus Christ, born of a woman, born under the Law, to redeem those who were under the Law, by dying on a Roman cross for the sins of the world (Gal. 4:4-5). At this point, we're given the opportunity to be brought back into the presence of God and to experience reconciliation and deliverance from our eternal separation from Him. The rescue is available only through Jesus, 'the way, the truth, and the life' (John 14:6). All we need to do is to accept God's gift of salvation and trust Christ, and Him alone, to be our Savior and Lord.

This is the movement in God's story—God's mission—in which we live out our lives and equip our children to do so today. The fourth and final movement, the *consummation* of this story, is yet to come. So, how does parenting fit into the biblical story? What does it have to do with the very mission of God?

Simply put, our mission is this: As Christian parents, we've been reconciled to God and are again able to live in God's spiritual presence through Christ and the Holy Spirit who lives in us. We're part of redeemed humanity, which is again enabled to make God known and to reflect His glory on this earth. How are we to do this: as generic individuals? No—as redeemed men and women who as married couples reproduce and procreate children who in turn need to be reconciled to their Creator and be taught about the wonderful salvation God provided when He sent His beloved Son to die for us on the Cross.

Our mission in making disciples—God's mission for us—starts in the home. Our first disciples should be our own children! If we neglect to prioritize this vital stewardship of discipling our children, little else we engage in will matter much for eternity. If we're not committed to making our families and homes a place of mission, then something is off-balance. Not that we should stop there—rightly understood, we should be Great Commission families, united in purpose, bonding together in love, embracing and fulfilling God's purpose for our lives individually and jointly, and consider ultimately *the church* is the family of God made up of those who are spiritually brothers and sisters in Christ. This constitutes a full-orbed understanding of the mission of God and of the way in which we participate in it.

The Mission of Parenting

Parenting, therefore, is more than merely training and disciplining your children for a productive life on earth. It's more than taking them to football practice, dance recitals, and music lessons. It's even more than taking them to church and memorizing a few (or plenty more) Bible verses (though that's a great start). Parenting, rightly understood, is *mission*. In fact, it's part of *God's* mission for the world, and specifically for you and your spouse. In bringing children into this world and in raising them to love and serve God, you are part of God's mission.

This involves nurturing Christlike character in our children rather than merely giving them an education, no matter how excellent. It also requires that we take a long view of God's purpose for them, so we won't get caught up in the daily minutiae but parent *responsibly*, with *purpose* and *perspective*. It requires acknowledging and adhering to the God-ordained roles for men and women, so that the mother can nurture her children and care for them while the father is encouraged to lead and provide for his family.

Helping Them Find Their Place in This World

God made each of us unique, with a certain set of gifts and a special calling. Like a Christmas present, this calling and these talents (and spiritual gifts upon conversion) are wrapped in a neat (or not so neat) little package which is your child. Usually we've found in our own lives is that what a child gravitates to early on ends up being central to their ministry and vocation later. Over the years, try to help them unpack that gift. Observe your child and see what he or she is good at. All of us are good at *something*! The joy is finding out what that is and then developing that gift, and we can help our children to excel in this.

Take our younger daughter as an example. As she grew and developed as a teenager, she showed an interest in healthy eating. She started reading about nutrition and discovered its value for physical well-being. As part of her interest in healthful diet, she encouraged us to buy healthier food. This wasn't part of any class or external influence, it was motivated by what was in her heart. She entered college in a generic field, not sure if she could handle the sciences, but still switched to nutrition, trusting God to enable her to succeed. She graduated with a Masters in Human Nutrition and started work in a hospital as a Registered Dietitian.

Things won't always be simple and straightforward, but if we're observant, we'll often be able to help our children discern their passions and drives in life and assist them in developing their gifts. Being able to find a vocation that they're good at and that they enjoy doing will be a tremendous blessing for them and those around them. This, of course, is an ongoing story. It's our hope that God will use our daughter's education and passion in the context of her family and in ministry to other families as well. We're waiting to see how God will develop her and our other children and in what direction he will take them in the years to come.

Natural and Spiritual Gifts

Speaking of giftedness, both of us believe that we should be careful not to disparage natural gifts in relation to spiritual gifts in the body of Christ. The same creator and Spirit gave us both. In fact, many natural gifts can be put to spiritual use once a person is converted and starts using their gifts for the benefit of others in the body of Christ. This is true for leadership gifts, such as teaching or administration. It's also true for service-related gifts, such as giving or mercy. Similarly, a person with musical gifting will be able to use their gift in a worship context. That said, a person must be *set apart for God's use*—something that is true for them spiritually at conversion but is worked out experientially over time—so they can exercise their spiritual gifts in a God-honoring and beneficial way in the local church.

What are your spiritual gifts? And what spiritual gifts do your children have? Do you know? Have you tried to help them determine what their spiritual gifts are and find appropriate places of ministry where they can exercise those gifts? How should we explore this with our children? What is an appropriate age? We readily concede that we ourselves may not always have done a very good job at that. In fact, it's sometimes hard to know what your gifts are until you start using them. Parents might start by determining and exercising their own gifts in the community of the church. In this way, you'll not only set the example but be better able to help your children as well.

Often the very best way to know what your gifts are is to step out in faith and get involved, or to ask other mature Christians who know you well. What do they perceive your strengths to be? How have they benefited from something you've done, perhaps without your even realizing it? Passing on a legacy of service in the church based on spiritual and natural gifting to your children may involve a cycle of *engagement* because they may not be ready or mature enough spiritually to explore their spiritual gifts at a given point in time. Every child has his or her own experience in life with God and pace of growth in maturity. As parents, we should follow the Spirit's leading in the context of our ongoing relationship with our children.

Preparing Our Children for Marriage

Just recently, I was led to ask myself the rather weighty question: How am I preparing my children for marriage? And how am I preparing them for service in the church? When we send our children to college for four years, that college will prepare them for all kinds of things (even things we wish they didn't). Marriage and serving in the church aren't among these and any messages they receive in this area might likely be contrary to what we would hope. And, what to do with that complicated experience of meeting and getting to know a person whom they might marry? That's where we as parents have an important role to play. Preparing our children for marriage, as well as serving God, must be a significant part of *our* vision for parenting. Many of us have embraced the notion that preparing for a vocation takes years of preparation, but marriage can be entered into on a whim if we just meet the 'right' person! Thus, many young people enter marriage unprepared, and often experience a rather rude awakening after the initial honeymoon phase is over (if not before or even during the honeymoon)!

One of the trickiest and most controversial subjects in Christian circles then is the question of *dating*. How are you supposed to meet your future spouse in a godly way? Should you shop around until you find the best available husband or wife? Is it simply a process of trial and error? How does your child know whether they and a potential spouse are compatible? And where is God in all of this? One school of thought holds that if the potential partner is a believer, it's up to you to decide. Others contend that God has one person for you to marry and you can trust Him to lead you to that person at His perfect time. The question is: Can you, and should you, trust God to lead you in this crucial area of life, or can you, and should you, trust yourself to make the right choices and go and find yourself a husband or wife? Or is it somehow a combination between the two ends of the spectrum?

It won't surprise you that we believe that God does indeed bring two people, a man and a woman, together to lead them into a relationship so they become husband and wife. God is the ultimate 'Matchmaker'! The book of Proverbs says that 'He who finds a wife finds what is good and receives favor from the LORD' (Prov. 18:22 NIV). As the God of providence, the God who sovereignly directs the affairs of men—and women, too—cares for every intimate detail of our lives, much more so about whom we will marry. As Peter writes in his first epistle, 'Cast all your anxieties on him because he cares for you' (1 Pet. 5:7 NIV). So what does it mean to trust God in this area of our lives? It means that we resist the urge to take matters into our own hands as parents, or as the one seeking God in this matter. We don't encourage manipulating others by flirting or aggressive behavior. Young men take appropriate Spirit-led initiative, while young women joyfully respond—or graciously resist—as they sense the Lord's leading (or lack thereof).

Clearly, the area of male-female relationships including a possible marriage relationship is too serious a matter to take out of God's hands into our own. We need to be careful to find the appropriate and responsible balance of influence in our children's lives in this area. Often the wisdom of parents is given insufficient weight while, at least in our experience, peers and even pastors (doubtless with good intentions) tend to take over. Cooperation and coordination between parents and pastors, however, can be helpful here. So be in touch with the college pastor if there is one. Instructing our children in this area of life involves helping them realize that God knows the end from the beginning; he will do what He knows is best.

At the same time, as in education, we as parents should take our responsibility seriously to guide our children in this very important matter. It seems vital to begin training and guiding them relatively early to help boys not to 'burn' with passion and turn to pornography because they are not married. Similarly, if girls wait too long to get married, they may be tempted to settle for a husband who is not a strong Christian partly out of loneliness. Remaining single for long may engender too much independence. The same goes for young men as well. The longer they wait, the more difficult it may be for them to be flexible and open to accommodate another person in their life.

We also need to be ready to discuss that in some rare cases, God may call a man or woman to remain unmarried so they can serve Him without being distracted by family responsibilities. But be clear that God will lead this way normally only if He gives them the gift ('charisma') of singleness (or celibacy). If your child shudders at the thought that they may have such a gift, chances are they don't! As a matter of fact, you can encourage them that from the beginning God created man and woman for each other for companionship and fruitfulness on purpose. It follows that God intends that most people marry. In any case, there are many ways in which God can bring a man and a woman together and confirm his leading in their lives.

Finding a Spouse

The Bible says that 'it is not good that the man should be alone' (Gen. 2:18). We believe that the same principle holds true for women, too. We were made for companionship, not aloneness, and can all attest to the fact that loneliness is a scourge, not a blessing. So, how should we look for a potential partner to share life with? Should Christians date? And if so, how? Or is what people sometimes label 'courtship' a better way to go? The difference between these two approaches is that in *dating* a man and a woman spend time together exclusively for a period to determine whether they're meant to get married while in *courtship* a commitment is made at the outset that a couple is pursuing the likelihood of marriage, having previously known each other in a larger social context such as church, college, family relationship, or friendship group.

What are the pros and cons of dating versus alternate approaches? Dating, especially dating at an early age, usually involves long periods of time spent together to determine compatibility. There may be a certain trial and error component in the process involved as well, as one would assume (though this is not necessarily an accurate assumption) that people gradually get smarter and learn what they need in another person to be fulfilled, until—so the theory goes—they eventually find 'The One.'

However, moving toward marriage is very different from shopping for shoes or some other item. Men and women are *people* with feelings and personalities, not inanimate objects! The extended time spent exclusively on dates may render young people vulnerable to sexual temptation when they aren't yet ready for marriage; as a result, one or both may get hurt in the process. Often much time and emotional energy are spent (wasted) that could have been used in the service of God. Other important and healthy relationships often become marginalized, much before a sole commitment is even necessary. Dating, or serial dating, may also have the potential of developing a relational habit of transience rather than one-person permanence and make it more difficult for a person eventually to settle down. And people—especially young women—may feel used or even used up in the process. You get the picture—we're not huge fans of unbridled dating!

The bottom line is that care and prayer should be taken in the process of getting to know the opposite sex. To counteract the potential negative entailments of dating, some favor an approach called 'courtship.' Yet this may be a bit reactionary and cause the pendulum to swing too far to the other extreme, from too flippant and casual an approach to one that gets too serious too soon. In fact, the courtship approach is uncomfortable for some because at times it requires young men to make a commitment to a woman (and vice versa) usually before he (and she) is ready or may not even know each other very well.

Personally, we encourage what you might call a 'friendship' approach which allows young adults time to get to know each other in larger and smaller group settings, hopefully in wholesome fellowshipping and in serving the Lord in local church ministry contexts amongst other things. If God leads a couple to recognize the potential for a special relationship beyond the friendship level, they may choose to go deeper, depending also on their age and stage in life. This cautious approach is helpful because it gives the opportunity for people to become acquainted without any pressure being placed on either person to commit before they know what they're getting themselves into.

Approaches to Finding a Life Partner

	Approach	Brief Description
1	Dating	Spending time together exclusively for a certain amount of time to enjoy the opposite sex, not always with the purpose of finding a marriage partner. Serial dating may ensue with several or many people, with or without the purpose of finding a marriage partner.

	Approach	Brief Description
2	Courtship	Commitment at the outset of spending time together (usually with parents' permission) that couple is pursuing marriage, also where time together involves accountability of an outside party.
3	Friendship	Young people get to know each other in larger and smaller group settings (or other informal ways) to form friendships before committing to a purposeful (likely to get married) but still exploratory relationship.

For reasons such as these, therefore, it likely seems best to proceed slowly until there's a growing and clear conviction that God may be at work. Be patient for God to bring someone across your path at the right time when both are ready to pursue a committed relationship. At that point, a young man may choose to initiate a relationship with a young woman when both are getting close to being ready for marriage, which—depending on circumstances, such as their age and the girl's parents' receptivity—may involve the young man's securing her father's permission to do so.

Also, encourage them to make the most of the time when they're not yet married. God is molding and shaping them into the persons he wants them to be. May God be glorified and may young women especially be protected in this delicate area of our lives. As in other areas, we should trust God to guide us, and He certainly will. As parents, we should impress on our children their need for wisdom and discernment in choosing a life partner. We should let them know that we respect their right to choose their own life partner but that we're available to give input whenever they're open to it and provide support whenever it's needed. We could also communicate that while the choice of a spouse is ultimately their decision, it does have obvious implications for the entire family.

On the one hand, we shouldn't uphold standards that are so high that no earthly being could ever attain to it—especially in their late teens or early twenties! On the other hand, we shouldn't hesitate to express concerns and reservations if they're well-founded, and hopefully our children will listen. If they believe that we have their best interests at heart, and that we want them to be happy, they'll realize that we're not trying to be obstructionist but rather drawing on decades of life experience from which they can benefit. If parents have been relational all along, being involved in this process won't be awkward but normal. Parental involvement is especially important with girls who, prior to marriage, would continue to benefit from the guidance and protection of their father.

Practical Tips

Our main advice for our children in seeking a spouse is to pray for the person God has designed for them and to discern a prospective life partner first, by the love he has for *God* and then by the love he has for *them*. Also, build solid *friendships*—even in marriage, a strong friendship is a lasting foundation for a strong marriage. In the meantime, help them to be patient and to keep pursuing that to which God has called them in terms of education and vocational preparation. Entering too quickly into a relationship from a point of desperation—not just need—not only has some of the above mentioned drawbacks but may render one unduly dependent on others and vulnerable to be taken advantage of.

As you pray for them and, as appropriate, advise them and provide a sounding board, help them to find someone who is compatible. By 'compatible' we mean *not* that they're the same but that they complement each other well. One may have a rather quiet personality and the other may be outgoing. In terms of age, calling, mission, interests, and even socioeconomic and cultural background, it's likely beneficial to have some similarities of background and, more importantly, calling. In any case, it's important to work through any differences and expectations for life, marriage, and family to avoid later difficulties in the context of lifelong commitment. It would be easy to dismiss these things when you are 'in love,' but the honeymoon won't last forever.

Always a Parent

You may think that parenting is over when you send your children off to college or even when they marry. However, we've found the opposite to be the case. It's exactly when you let your children go and they experience the freedom that comes with college life that they often realize that they need and desire parental and others' input, so they can make good decisions in a variety of areas. Few young people are fully prepared for everything when they leave for college despite your best efforts to equip them for life. They may contact you and want to talk to you about struggles in relationships, ask for your help in developing study skills, or want you to give advice on that first job interview or subsequent ones. This, of course, presupposes that you have cultivated the kind of relationship with them while they were at home that engendered trust and conveyed to them a sense that you love them in the way very few others do or ever will.

So, don't look at parenting as something that will end when your kids go off to college or at some other time. If you're a father or mother, you'll always be a father or mother. The nature of your relationship with your children will change over time, and will most likely turn into a close friendship, if all goes well. But there'll always be a sense in which you can provide guidance and share your life experience with the next generation. In fact, that's why we wrote this book. Thanks so much for joining us for a few brief moments on our parenting journey, and every blessing as you, as parents, are about God's mission to make disciples of children who will reflect His glory on earth and tell others about Him.

Conclusion

As responsible parents who nurture and equip their children with perspective and purpose along the entire life cycle of parenting, one of our greatest joys and challenges is to equip our children for their mission in life. In doing so, a solid grasp of the mission of God as conveyed in the biblical storyline will be indispensable. Based on understanding the four movements in the divine symphony of creating and redeeming a people for God, we'll be able to assist our children in finding their mission and purpose in life, including their service in the local church. Be a perceptive observer and a good listener of your children. Every child is different and individually fashioned by God with unique gifts and a tailor-made calling.

The mystery is that we have a sovereign, transcendent God who is at the same time concerned for every detail of our lives (including our marriage partner!).

What makes things more intriguing and at times more perplexing is that God normally reveals His will for us as part of a process rather than all at once. This requires many small steps of obedience and responses along the way. We must follow Him in what He has already revealed to us or we can't expect Him to reveal what He wants us to do in the future. We must keep in step with God as we walk through life with Him. In the Bible, we read about believers who 'walked with God' for dozens and in some cases even hundreds of years (Gen. 5:24). Can you imagine the intimacy that comes from living life closely aligned with another person? Those of us who have been married for twenty or more years can appreciate the transformative power and potential of this kind of union.

May we walk closely with Him and with each other throughout our parenting journey, and may we inspire our children to do the same.

♦ *Considering what was said about finding our mission in view of God's mission, is there anything you need to change regarding your perspective on your role as a parent in your child's life? If so, what kinds of changes do you need to make?*

♦ *Have you identified your own God-given mission in life? If so, are you modeling this God-given mission in front of your children? What is your mission in life, and how do you know?*

♦ *What, would you say, is your children's mission in life, one by one? How much progress have you and they made in discovering God's purpose for their lives?*

RECOMMENDED RESOURCES

Andreas Köstenberger. *Excellence: The Character of God and the Pursuit of Scholarly Virtue.* Wheaton: Crossway, 2011.

Andreas Köstenberger with David Jones. *God, Marriage, and Family: Rebuilding the Biblical Foundation.* Second edition. Wheaton: Crossway, 2010. Abridged as *Marriage and the Family: Biblical Essentials.* Wheaton: Crossway, 2012.

Andreas and Margaret Köstenberger. *God's Design for Man and Woman: A Biblical-Theological Survey.* Wheaton: Crossway, 2014. Also available in course format at www.biblemesh.com and www.biblicalfoundations.org: *God's Design for Man and Woman* (full course), *Man and Woman: Biblical Essentials* (abridged course).

Candice Watters. *Get Married: What Women Can Do to Help It Happen.* Chicago: Moody, 2008.

Dennis and Barbara Rainey. *Passport2Purity.* Little Rock, AR: FamilyLife, 2012.

Dennis and Barbara Rainey and others. *Passport2Identity for Young Men. Passport2Identity for Young Women.* Little Rock, AR: FamilyLife, 2016.

Dennis Rainey. *Stepping Up: A Call to Courageous Manhood.* Little Rock, AR: FamilyLife, 2011.

Gloria Furman. *Glimpses of Grace: Treasuring the Gospel in Your Home.* Wheaton: Crossway, 2013.

Gloria Furman. *Missional Motherhood: The Everyday Ministry of Motherhood in the Grand Plan of God.* Wheaton: Crossway, 2016.

Gloria Furman. *Treasuring Christ When Your Hands Are Full: Gospel Meditations for Busy Moms.* Wheaton: Crossway, 2014.

Ken Sande, with Tom Raabe. *Peacemaking for Families: A Biblical Guide to Managing Conflict in Your Home.* Wheaton: Tyndale, 2002.

Margaret Köstenberger. *Sanctification.* The Good Portion. Fearn, Ross-shire: Christian Focus, forthcoming.

Marshall Segal. *Not Yet Married: The Pursuit of Joy in Singleness and Dating.* Wheaton: Crossway, 2017.

Paul David Tripp. *Age of Opportunity: A Biblical Guide to Parenting Teens.* Second edition. Phillipsburg, NJ: P&R, 2001.

Steve and Candice Watters. *Start Your Family: Inspiration for Having Babies.* Chicago: Moody, 2009.

Tedd Tripp. *Shepherding a Child's Heart.* Revised and updated edition. Wapwallopen, PA: Shepherd, 1995.

www.biblicalfoundations.org. *This website features articles, blogs, videos, and other resources on marriage and family, as well as other relevant topics.*

Christian Focus Publications

Our mission statement —

STAYING FAITHFUL
In dependence upon God we seek to impact the world through literature faithful to His infallible Word, the Bible. Our aim is to ensure that the Lord Jesus Christ is presented as the only hope to obtain forgiveness of sin, live a useful life and look forward to heaven with Him.

Our books are published in four imprints:

CHRISTIAN
FOCUS

Popular works including biographies, commentaries, basic doctrine and Christian living.

CHRISTIAN
HERITAGE

Books representing some of the best material from the rich heritage of the church.

MENTOR

Books written at a level suitable for Bible College and seminary students, pastors, and other serious readers. The imprint includes commentaries, doctrinal studies, examination of current issues and church history.

CF4•K

Children's books for quality Bible teaching and for all age groups: Sunday school curriculum, puzzle and activity books; personal and family devotional titles, biographies and inspirational stories – because you are never too young to know Jesus!

Christian Focus Publications Ltd,
Geanies House, Fearn, Ross-shire,
IV20 1TW, Scotland, United Kingdom.
www.christianfocus.com
blog.christianfocus.com